WOMEN OF THE OLD TESTAMENT

Their Lives, Our Hope

PÍA SEPTIÉN

Liguori
Liguori, Missouri

Imprimi Potest:
Harry Grile, CSsR, Provincial
Denver Province, The Redemptorists

Published by Liguori Publications
Liguori, MO 63057-9999

To order, call 800-325-9521, or visit liguori.org.

Library of Congress Cataloging-in-Publication Data

Septién, Pía.
[Las Mujeres del Antiguo Testamento. English]
The women of the Old Testament : their lives, our hope / Pía Septién.—1st ed.
p. cm.
Includes bibliographical references and index.
ISBN 978-0-7648-2204-9 (alk. paper)
1. Women in the Bible—Meditations. 2. Bible. O.T.—Meditations. 3. Catholic Church—Prayers and devotions. I. Title.

BS575.S4213 2012
221.9'22—dc23

2012003629

Liguori Publications, a nonprofit corporation, is an apostolate of The Redemptorists. To learn more about The Redemptorists, visit Redemptorists.com.

Printed in the United States of America.
20 19 18 17 16 / 6 5 4 3 2

CONTENTS

For my husband, César,

who helps me keep

my feet on the ground

and my eyes set on heaven.

INTRODUCTION

The book you are holding, as its title indicates, is about women whose names and stories appear in the Old Testament. Some will be quite familiar to you, such as Ruth, Anna, Miriam, and Abigail. Wonderful! And perhaps this will be your chance to meet other women whose stories are not as well-known, such as Leah, Michal, Hagar, Shiphrah, and Puah. All of them have important lessons to teach us.

Although thousands of years have gone by since they were written about, their lives are as current for us as today's news. Why? Because God—with his presence and care, providence and love—was present in their lives then just as he is in ours today. Like them, we live in a world where we face all kinds of good and bad experiences.

Like us, they experienced anger, joy, indignation, happiness. Perhaps they needed to leave their homeland to look for new horizons and opportunities, tried to be faithful to God, served their fellow men, could not have children, took care of their mothers-in-law and unborn babies, prayed, were widowed, or were used and abused. Their story is our story.

The purpose of this book is for us to learn about their lives, reflect about them, delve deeply into them, and assimilate all that they have to teach us.

They resemble us in their times of strength, and their weaknesses consumed them just as they consume us. Thus do their lives become our hope.

The book is divided into ten chapters, each of which is dedicated to the Old Testament women on whom we will be focusing. Within each chapter you will find a brief introduction to the character(s), scriptural citations, the biblical story told at greater length, and the different lessons—both positive and negative—that we learn about the women. We feature teachings from the *Catechism of the Catholic Church* related to the topic, questions to foster personal reflection, and group activities to tie up some ideas or possible resolutions to bring what we learned to others and so make our family, community, and world a better place.

I recommend you read it on an individual level or study it as a group. I wrote it this way because the world needs us to reflect, not just to repeat others' ideas. We need to be able to delve deeply into a topic, analyze it, draw conclusions, and act upon the resolutions we set for ourselves.

And now, I leave you in the company of eleven Old Testament women.

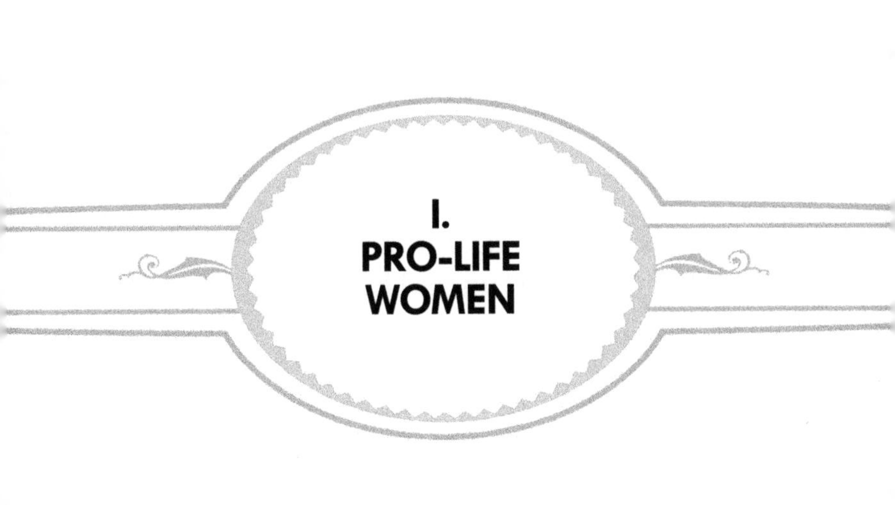

I. PRO-LIFE WOMEN

CHAPTER 1

RUTH

A good daughter-in-law and faithful friend

"A 'charity that is kind' not only knows how to 'see' the 'other' but opens itself to him, seeks him out, reaches out to him. Love gives generously. [...] And how often do we close ourselves within the shell of our 'I,' not knowing, not wanting, not trying to open ourselves to the 'other,' to give him something of our own 'I,' going beyond the limits of our self-centeredness or perhaps selfishness, and striving to become men, women 'for others,' like Christ."

Homily of Pope John Paul II
Pastoral Visit to the Roman Parish of the Ascension
February 3, 1980

Objective

In a society where the elderly and some other social or family relationships are seen as a burden, Ruth presents herself to us as a loving woman able to meet the needs of her mother-in-law, Naomi. At the same time, we see God's loving care for two widows, Ruth and Naomi.

Let us take a deeper look at a Bible story where we see the reality of human life; that is, in human life there are difficult moments, but there are also moments of great joy. Here we touch on themes central to human life: abandonment, solitude, sadness, old age, dependence. At the same time, we see acts of friendship, loyalty, hope, and finally, of salvation.

As we read about Ruth's life at the mercy of circumstances in the company of her mother-in-law, Naomi, and as we learn about her "comings and goings," her sufferings and joys, we will be able to see an image of our own life in hers.

Scripture text: *Ruth 1–4*

Introduction to the character

Who was Ruth?

Ruth was a Moabite woman, which means she came from a territory east of the Dead Sea. Today that territory is Jordan. She married a Hebrew named Mahlon, who had come to Moab with his parents when they fled the famine that swept across Bethlehem of Judah, their native land. With the passage of time, her husband died and she stayed close to her mother-in-law, Naomi, who was also a widow and whose two sons had died.

When Naomi heard there was food again in her native land, she decided to return. Not wanting to leave her alone, Ruth returned with her.

According to Hebrew law, Ruth and Naomi, both childless widows, were to be the responsibility of the nearest relative, known as *goel*. This word means "redeemer." The redeemer was obligated to help his needy relatives and also had the right to claim the patrimony his relatives may have lost. That is how Ruth came into contact with Boaz, a relative of her husband. Boaz, who appreciated Ruth's loyalty to Naomi, allowed her to glean barley and wheat in his field and instructed his workers not to trouble her.

The story tells us about the legal arrangements Boaz made to exercise his right to act as Ruth's *goel*. And—what a surprise—he ended up marrying her. They had a son together named Obed, who would one day be the grandfather of King David.

Development of the Bible story

Ruth's story begins like many stories of human lives—with the need to leave her own land, the place where she was born and grew up, to seek out a better life. The Book of Ruth tells us how there was a famine in the land of Bethlehem. This famine forced Elimelech to take his wife, Naomi, and his two sons, Mahlon and Chilion, and leave the land of Moab.

To the tragedy of having to leave their own land, a second was added: the death of Naomi's husband, Elimelech. The sons married Moabite women, Ruth and Orpah. This may seem logical and peaceful to the modern reader, but it was not so for the fifth century BC Hebrew culture in which the brothers lived.

The story tells us how the brothers died after ten years, leaving their wives widowed and childless. Things get even more complicated, since now there are three widowed women: Naomi, Ruth, and Orpah, none of whom had children. It is worth noting that in that society, the husband and male children were indispensable for survival, since they took charge of watching over the well-being of their wives, mothers, sisters, and daughters.

The three women form a community to survive in a society in which they have no security, freedom, or certainty. Their future is uncertain, unless one of them should remarry. Naomi, Ruth, and Orpah create a community like those that have been formed throughout the history of humanity. Today we are part of communities in which we are united by bonds or interests like our family, our extended family, our group of friends or neighbors, the community of the Church, etc. In a way, we also seek to survive.

The time of famine had ended in Bethlehem of Judah, so Naomi opts to return to her own land with Ruth and Orpah. Halfway there, Naomi decides it is not fair to ask the two young women to leave their families, their land, and the possibility of remarrying and having children in order to follow her, so she urges them to return home to their mothers.

At first, the response of both women is, "We will go back with you, to your people." But later, Orpah, in tears, decides to return to her family. Blessed freedom, God's great gift to humanity, allowed Orpah and Ruth, as well as us, to follow the voice of conscience. Orpah returns home while Ruth stays with Naomi. We could fall into the temptation of judging Orpah as a selfish person. If so, our judgment would be very harsh. Do we know what trials she was going through in her heart? Do we know the difficulties she was facing? Perhaps Orpah was simply seeking the security of what was familiar, her family and ordinary life as she knew it.

And so we find the world has women like Orpah who live an ordinary life, spending their days, months, and years in anonymity, without doing anything that makes it into the newspapers or is recorded in books. Those women are faithful to their daily work; it is hidden, barely noticed by others, and yet so necessary, truly heroic. That constant, quiet work is what builds up the family, society, and—ultimately—the world.

But just as we need many Orpahs in the world, we also need

decisive, brave, and enterprising women like Ruth. These are the women who launch important initiatives, who "put it all on the line," women who are able to follow the voice of their conscience inviting them to do good, no matter the cost.

Ruth's story shows us the greatness of an unselfish and generous human love capable of forgetting self so as to give to others, even when "the others" are not of the same age, race, religion, or culture. It is love that overcomes the limitations created by human beings and makes us see how hard suffering, the loss of loved ones, and affliction can be. That is what we see in Ruth when she tells Naomi:

> "Do not press me to go back and abandon you! Wherever you go I will go, wherever you lodge I will lodge. Your people shall be my people and your God, my God. Where you die I will die, and there be buried."
>
> RUTH 1:16–17A

Naomi and Ruth return to Bethlehem in the midst of their distressing reality. Ruth has lost not only her husband but also her country and her family. Naomi, for her part, has lost her husband, her two sons, and the possibility of having grandchildren. Added to that is the fact that neither of them has a man to take care of them. So great is Naomi's sorrow that she expresses it openly upon arriving in Bethlehem:

> So they went on together until they reached Bethlehem. On their arrival there, the whole town was excited about them, and the women asked: "Can this be Naomi?" But she said to them, "Do not call me Naomi ['Sweet']. Call me Mara ['Bitter'], for the Almighty has made my life very bitter. I went away full, but the LORD has brought me back empty. Why should you call me 'Sweet,' since the LORD has brought me to trial, and the Almighty has pronounced evil sentence on me."
>
> RUTH 1:19–21

There is one more lesson in this story: Each person bears pain in a different way. Naomi is open and frank in the way she expresses her pain, while Ruth is more discreet. In fact, the book tells us absolutely nothing about her feelings, even after her husband dies and she leaves her land. We see how one woman shares her sorrow with others and the other keeps it all inside. Let us learn to respect the way others bear their sufferings, although this does not mean we leave them all alone. We must accompany them without overwhelming them.

Once in Bethlehem, the two widowed women have only one option to survive: to glean grain in the fields where the harvest is being collected. The Hebrew law stipulated that part of the harvest should be left behind so that the poor could gather it. Ruth asks her mother-in-law to allow her to glean grain in the field. Was it coincidence or divine providence that Ruth unknowingly went to glean grain in the field of Boaz, a rich relative of her deceased husband?

Boaz asks the young man overseeing his harvesters, "Whose young woman is this?" The young man overseeing the harvesters answers, "She is the young Moabite who came back with Naomi from the plateau of Moab. She said, 'I would like to gather the gleanings into sheaves after the harvesters.' Ever since she came this morning she has remained here until now, with scarcely a moment's rest." Boaz then speaks to Ruth, "Listen, my daughter. Do not go to glean in anyone else's field; you are not to leave here. Stay here with my young women. Watch to see which field is to be harvested, and follow them. Have I not commanded the young men to do you no harm? When you are thirsty, go and drink from the vessels the young people have filled" (Ruth 2:5–9).

When Ruth asks Boaz why he has been so generous with her, Boaz answers that he has heard how generous she has been with Naomi. He also tells her that she has reached the land of Bethlehem, the land of the God of Israel, under whose protection she now lives:

> "May the LORD reward what you have done! May you receive a full reward from the LORD, the God of Israel, under whose wings you have come for refuge."
>
> RUTH 2:12

For her part, Naomi perceives God's hand in all of these events:

> "May he be blessed by the LORD, who never fails to show kindness to the living and to the dead," Naomi exclaimed to her daughter-in-law. She continued, "This man is a near relative of ours, one of our redeemers."
>
> RUTH 2:20

Both recognize the presence of God in the midst of the events. Are we able to recognize God's presence in our lives?

Continuing with the story, Naomi hatches an unusual plan to get Ruth and Boaz to marry! Women certainly have the initiative and capacity to put the wildest plans into action when we think it is necessary:

> Naomi said to her, "My daughter, should I not be seeking a pleasing home for you? Now! Is not Boaz, whose young women you were working with, a relative of ours? This very night he will be winnowing barley at the threshing floor. Now, go bathe and anoint yourself; then put on your best attire and go down to the threshing floor. Do not make yourself known to the man before he has finished eating and drinking. But when he lies down, take note of the place where he lies; then go uncover a place at his feet and you lie down. He will then tell you what to do."
>
> RUTH 3:1–4

We see how the characters plan and act, trusting in the goodness of others. Naomi hopes that Boaz will act like a gentleman and marry Ruth, and Ruth hopes that her mother-in-law is not wrong. The same happens in our lives. A time comes when things cannot continue the way they are going and we must take action. At those times, we need to make decisions and trust in God and others.

The rest of Ruth's story unfolds within intricate legal complications having to do with the rights that a closer relative had to buy Naomi's field and marry Ruth. In the end, this right falls to Boaz.

Upon seeing that the right is his, Boaz says to all those present:

> "You are witnesses today that I have acquired from Naomi all the holdings of Elimelech, Chilion and Mahlon. I also acquire Ruth the Moabite, the widow of Mahlon, as my wife, in order to raise up a family for her late husband on his estate, so that the name of the deceased may not perish from his people and his place. Do you witness this today?"
>
> RUTH 4:9–10

What began as a tragedy ends happily with the wedding of Ruth and Boaz and the birth of Obed. For Naomi, the baby boy is the joy of her old age; for Boaz, he is the son who will allow his lineage to continue; for Elimelech, he is the guarantee that his memory will be immortalized; for the people of Israel, he is the grandfather of their beloved King David. And Obed gives Ruth a place in the genealogy of Jesus, who has us remember her every time we read the Gospel of Matthew:

> The book of the genealogy of Jesus Christ, the son of David, the son of Abraham. Abraham became the father of Isaac, Isaac the father of Jacob, Jacob the father of Judah and his brothers. Judah became the father of Perez and Zerah, whose mother was Tamar. Perez became the father of Hezron, Hezron the father of Ram, Ram the father of Amminadab. Amminadab became the father of Nahshon, Nahshon the father of Salmon, Salmon the father of Boaz,

> whose mother was Rahab. Boaz became the father of Obed, whose mother was Ruth. Obed became the father of Jesse, Jesse the father of David the king.
>
> MATTHEW 1:1–6A

The story of Ruth ends by showing us what teamwork can do: together, Ruth, Naomi, and Boaz manage to continue the line of descent. And there, behind the scenes, we can see the loving action of God as he watches over his people.

What does Ruth teach us?

The Book of Ruth is made up of only four chapters, but within those short chapters we find many lessons:

- It tells us a story that begins with a famine, departure from the land where the family lived before, and then the death of a husband. However, the story ends with a marriage, the birth of a son, and the recovery of the land. It proves the saying, "No evil lasts forever."
- It depicts the hardships a family had to endure in order to survive in adversity.
- It shows us how loving dedication comes about when we put others' needs before our own.
- It demonstrates that every decision is a new opportunity to do good.
- It shows us how Ruth and Naomi had to make decisions in difficult circumstances while being hemmed in by situations of poverty, solitude, and abandonment.
- It confirms something we already know but that we need to remember: No matter how hard the circumstances may be and no matter how hard things may seem, we have to act! We cannot stand around with our arms crossed. Ruth and Naomi acted. There is a common saying, "If life gives you lemons, make lemonade." They made lemonade with the lemons they had at hand.

- It teaches us that if we want to have a human relationship that is worthwhile, that lasts for many long years and that prevails through all difficulties, everyone involved has to contribute his part. Every relationship requires commitment, fidelity, and loyalty.
- It shows us the relationship between two women who walk together through good times and bad: in marriages, in the deaths of their husbands, in the move to another land, in poverty, in their work to subsist, in remarriage, and in the birth of a baby.
- It teaches us the importance of the community to be able to live and, sometimes, even in order to survive.
- It prepares us to understand suffering better and that even though it may lead us through confusing and chaotic situations, it makes us more human, more sensitive to others' needs, less critical, and of course, more grateful.
- It shows us how there is always hope, even when all seems lost.
- It speaks to us of the sorrows that come up unexpectedly in our lives and of the people who help us in tough times when all seems lost.
- We see how the relationship between the two women continues, even when one of them has married Boaz. We see how the good fortune of one woman does not become the other's downfall. Quite the opposite—the blessing Ruth obtained by gaining a husband and a child becomes Naomi's chance to have a family.

What does the *Catechism of the Catholic Church* tell us?

§1604: "God who created man out of love also calls him to love the fundamental and innate vocation of every human being. For man is created in the image and likeness of God (Genesis 1:2) who is himself love (see 1 John 4:8, 16). Since God created [them] man and woman, their mutual love becomes an image of the absolute and unfailing love with which God loves man. It is good, very good, in the Creator's eyes (see Genesis 1:31). And this love which God blesses is intended to be fruitful and to be realized in the common work of watching over creation: 'And God blessed them, and God said to them: "Be fruitful and multiply, and fill the earth and subdue it"' (Genesis 1:28).

§1730: God created man a rational being.

§1731: Freedom is the power to perform deliberate actions on one's own responsibility.

§1738: Every human person has the natural right to be recognized as a free and responsible being.

§1747: Every person has the right to the exercise of freedom, especially in religious and moral matters.

§1935: The equality of men rests essentially on their dignity as persons.

Questions for personal reflection

- What does friendship mean to me?
- What qualities do my friends have? What do I like about them?
- What are the characteristics of the people I can't stand to be around?
- Do I see in my life the loving hand of God, who gives me my "daily bread?"
- Have I ever had a friendship with someone like the friendship between Ruth and Naomi? A friendship that has gone through joyful times and hard times?
- Have I ever taken advantage of a friendship? What can I do to make up for the wrong I did to that person?
- Has a person who called herself my friend ever taken advantage of me? How did I feel then? How do I feel about it now?

- How do I treat the elderly people around me? Am I patient with them? Do I help them? Do they find support in me or a bad attitude?
- Have I seen God's loving hand in my life? When and how?
- Do I live at peace, trusting that God holds me in the palm of his hand, as the prophet Isaiah says (Isaiah 49:16)?

Group questions and activities

- What have you learned from Ruth? From Naomi? From Boaz?
- What do they teach you about friendship, loyalty, and trust? Which of these virtues is lived most in your times and which is more particular to the time of Ruth?
- List the different ways you can show love and kindness to:
  - Your family
  - Your friends
  - Colleagues at work
  - Relatives
  - The people who serve you in a store, a restaurant, etc.
- The mass media, such as television or the Internet, can lead you to isolate yourself from others and live enclosed in your own little world. Is that good? Why or why not? What would be the best way to use those media?
- Have you had to leave your land in search of a better life? Explain.
- What has been your experience upon joining a community? Was it good, ordinary, or bad? Why?
- Is there anyone in your life who has helped you through tough times? How?
- Have you helped anyone through tough times?
- What happens when there is no simple solution to what you are living?

- Describe a time when you experienced the loving hand of God in your life.
- Make a list of the different ways you can help the elderly.

Practical resolutions

What does all of the above call me to do?

- To give thanks to God for my daily bread, saying the prayer, "Thank you, Lord, for life and sustenance. You give it to me because of who you are, not because I deserve it" or some other prayer that shows our gratitude.
- To remember that God is present around me and within me.
- To invite God into my conversations, decisions, and plans.
- To keep in mind that God sent Jesus to show me his loving face and that his love is so absolute that the Holy Spirit lives in my heart.
- To pray for those who have had to leave home, land, and fam-ily in search of a better life.
- To avoid getting angry when people do not do things the way I like.
- To treat the elderly with patience and to help them in their needs.
- To seek out someone from whom I am estranged and to do everything I can to heal the rift.
- To participate actively in the life of my community, whether it be my family, work, the Church, etc.
- To thank God for the people who have been loyal to me and my family, especially in hard times. To pray for them.
- To ask God for the light and strength I need to see who needs my help.
- To hope against all hope, trusting in God.

Prayer

Benedictus

Blessed be the Lord, the God of Israel,
for he has visited and brought redemption to his people.
He has raised up a horn for our salvation
within the house of David his servant,
even as he promised through the mouth of his holy
prophets from of old:
salvation from our enemies and from the hand
of all who hate us,
to show mercy to our fathers
and to be mindful of his holy covenant
and of the oath he swore to Abraham our father,
and to grant us that,
rescued from the hand of enemies,
without fear we might worship him
in holiness and righteousness
before him all our days.
And you, child, will be called prophet of the Most High,
for you will go before the Lord to prepare his ways,
to give his people knowledge of salvation
through the forgiveness of their sins,
because of the tender mercy of our God
by which the daybreak from on high will visit us
to shine on those who sit in darkness and death's shadow,
to guide our feet into the path of peace.

LUKE 1:68–79

CHAPTER 2

SHIPHRAH and PUAH

Women who truly grasped the value of human life

"Before I formed you in the womb I knew you, before you were born I dedicated you."

JEREMIAH 1:5

"Can a mother forget her infant, be without tenderness for the child of her womb? Even should she forget, I will never forget you. See, upon the palms of my hands I have engraved you."

ISAIAH 49:15–16A

Human life must be respected and protected absolutely from the moment of conception. From the first moment of his existence, a human being must be recognized as having the rights of a person—among which is the inviolable right of every innocent being to life.

CONGREGATION FOR THE DOCTRINE OF THE FAITH,
INSTRUCTION *DONUM VITAE* I,1

Objective

In a society where the mass media and the opinions of the "powerful" seem to influence everything, it is worth reflecting on how these two women were capable of defying the orders of the powerful Egyptian Pharaoh so as to defend human life.

Scriptural text: *Exodus 1:15–19*

Introduction to the characters

Who were Shiphrah and Puah?

Shiphrah and Puah were two women who lived in Egypt, midwives who dedicated themselves to caring for Hebrew women as they gave birth, and who received an order from the Pharaoh to let the newborn babies die if they were males. But they did not follow the order because they feared God.

Development of the Bible story

The first thing we can say about these two courageous women is that the only reference to them and their actions in all of sacred Scripture is in the first five verses at the beginning of the Book of Exodus. That is all. There is not a single mention after that, but their bravery made their names and memories last for many generations.

To be able to appreciate the courage of these two women and the reason why they received such an odd order from the Egyptian Pharaoh, we must go back into history and understand how the Hebrew people got to this moment.

In order to do so, we have to go to the Book of Genesis, which recounts how the sons of Jacob, belonging to the Hebrew people, sell their brother Joseph—because they were envious of him—to a caravan of merchants. The merchants bring him to Egypt, where he is sold as a slave.

Starting in chapter thirty-nine, Genesis tells us how Joseph wins the favor of the king of Egypt, called "Pharaoh," by interpreting his dreams about an epoch of abundant harvests, followed by an epoch of famine. Because he interpreted the dreams successfully, the Pharaoh tells Joseph, "Since God has made all this known to you, there is no one as discerning and wise as you are. You shall be in charge of my household, and all my people will obey your command. Only in respect to the throne will I outrank you" (Genesis 41:39–40).

As time goes by, Joseph continues faithfully serving the Pharaoh, building silos to store the abundant harvests and thus be able to face the approaching times of scarcity. Once those times arrive, famine spreads throughout the region, which makes Jacob, Joseph's father, send his sons to buy grain in the land of Egypt.

When Joseph's brothers stand before him (now Egypt's governor) to buy food, he recognizes them, but they do not recognize him. Once Joseph sees sincere repentance in his brothers, he tells them:

> "I am your brother Joseph, whom you sold into Egypt. But now do not be distressed, and do not be angry with yourselves for having sold me here. It was really for the sake of saving lives that God sent me here ahead of you. The famine has been in the land for two years now, and for five more years cultivation will yield no harvest. God, therefore, sent me on ahead of you to ensure for you a remnant on earth and to save your lives in an extraordinary deliverance. So it was not really you but God who had me come here; and he has made me a father to Pharaoh, lord of all his household, and ruler over the whole land of Egypt. Hurry back, then, to my father and tell him: 'Thus says your son Joseph: God has made me lord of all Egypt; come down to me without delay.'"
>
> Genesis 45:4–9

Joseph settles his father and brothers in Egypt and, following Pharaoh's orders, gives them a plot of land in the best part of the Ramses region, providing them with everything they need to live on.

The story of the Hebrew people, made up of Joseph, his father, his brothers, and all his descendants, continues in the land of Egypt, where they settle and multiply. The years and centuries go by and, not surprisingly, the Egyptians gradually forget who Joseph was and what he had done for them. Thus Joseph and his people—the Hebrew people—become unwanted by the Egypt-ians.

Sacred Scripture tells us, "Then a new king, who knew nothing of Joseph, rose to power in Egypt. He said to his people, 'See! The Israelite people have multiplied and become more numerous than we are! Come, let us deal shrewdly with them to stop their increase; otherwise, in time of war they too may join our enemies to fight against us'" (Exodus 1:8–10).

It is under these circumstances that the Pharaoh of Egypt turns to the midwives who work with the Hebrews Shiphrah and Puah and tells them, "When you act as midwives for the Hebrew women, look on the birthstool: if it is a boy, kill him; but if it is a girl, she may live" (Exodus 1:16).

What a royal order! "The midwives, however, feared God; they did not do as the king of Egypt had ordered them, but let the boys live" (Exodus 1:17). As an excuse, they say that the Hebrew women are stronger than Egyptian women and that they gave birth before the midwives could arrive to attend them.

What courageous women! They fear God and act accordingly. Their temporal master orders them to take life away, but they do not follow his orders, knowing that life comes from the eternal Lord and Creator. They are a true example of pro-life women.

What do Shiphrah and Puah teach us?

- To respect the lives of the unborn.
- To defend life, no matter the cost.
- Not to let ourselves be overcome by circumstances, no matter how bad it gets. God is more powerful.
- To understand that God is God.
- To work for life in a committed way.
- To help young women who are pregnant.
- To help the most vulnerable in society.
- To join support groups that help women who have gone through an abortion, remembering always that God is merciful.
- The importance of being faithful to our own conscience, even under difficult circumstances, as in the case of Shiphrah and Puah, who received Pharaoh's order not to let the Hebrew baby boys live.

What does the *Catechism of the Catholic Church* tell us?

§2258: "Human life is sacred because from its beginning it involves the creative action of God and it remains forever in a special relationship with the Creator, who is its sole end. God alone is the Lord of life from its beginning until its end: no one can under any circumstance claim...the right directly to destroy an innocent human being" (CDF, instruction *Donum vitae* intro. 5).

§2260: Life is a gift from God.

§2270: Life must be protected from the moment of conception.

§2273: Society has the duty to protect life.

§1778: "Conscience is a judgment of reason whereby the human person recognizes the moral quality of a concrete act that he is going to perform, is in the process of performing, or has already completed."

§1782: Man has the right to act according to his conscience.

§1783–1785: The formation of conscience.

§1786–1789: Decisions must be made according to conscience.

Questions for personal reflection

- Do I understand that human life is sacred from the moment of conception to natural death?
- What is my attitude toward human life? Am I concerned about the international campaigns and movements to trample life?
- Following up on the previous question, what can I do concretely to take part in the battle to defend life all over the world?
- Do I look for some way to help those in need? Do I strive to be a light in others' lives?
- Am I aware that I have to make many decisions every day, from the moment my alarm clock goes off to the words I say and the criticisms that I avoid saying? And do I realize that many things depend on these decisions: the happiness of other people and my own happiness, health, well-being, etc.? Do I make these decisions consciously or superficially?
- Have I reflected on the importance of having a well-formed conscience that always tends toward the good?
- What place does God occupy in my life? When I make decisions, do I invite him to come with me?

Group questions and activities

- Look into pro-life activities that are going on in the diocese and see which of those activities you could participate in.
- Meet to knit or sew an outfit that can be donated to a center that helps single mothers who have chosen to keep their babies.
- Pray a rosary together for the pro-life cause.

- Reflect as a group on the parable of the prodigal son, which is in Luke 15:11–31. The purpose of this activity is to examine the father's loving attitude toward his two sons. Keep in mind that in this parable, the father is an image of God, who is merciful and always waiting with open arms for his sons to come home.

The parable says the younger son had squandered his inheritance, and that upon seeing himself in need, he decides:

> "'I shall get up and go to my father and I shall say to him, "Father, I have sinned against heaven and against you. I no longer deserve to be called your son; treat me as you would treat one of your hired workers."' So he got up and went back to his father. While he was still a long way off, his father caught sight of him, and was filled with compassion. He ran to his son, embraced him and kissed him. His son said to him, 'Father, I have sinned against heaven and against you; I no longer deserve to be called your son.' But his father ordered his servants, 'Quickly bring the finest robe and put it on him; put a ring on his finger and sandals on his feet. Take the fattened calf and slaughter it. Then let us celebrate with a feast, because this son of mine was dead, and has come to life again; he was lost, and has been found.' [...] Now the older son had been out in the field and, on his way back, as he neared the house, he heard the sound of music and dancing. [...] He asked what this might mean. The servant said to him, 'Your brother has returned and your father has slaughtered the fattened calf because he has him back safe and sound.' He became angry, and when he refused to enter the house, his father came out and pleaded with him. [...] 'My son, you are here with me always; everything I have is yours. But now we must celebrate and rejoice, because your brother was dead and has come to life again; he was lost and has been found.'"
>
> Luke 15:18–32

Analyze this text in depth and identify the three ideas that you consider most important:

> "Deep within their consciences men and women discover a law which they have not laid upon themselves and which they must obey. Its voice, ever calling them to love and to do what is good and to avoid evil, tells them inwardly at the right moment: do this, shun that" (Pastoral Constitution on the Church in the Modern World [*Gaudium et spes*], 16).

Practical resolutions

- Volunteer in a clinic that helps women who are considering having an abortion to help women decide to keep their babies.
- Pray in front of an abortion clinic.
- Participate in diocesan pro-life projects.
- Pray every day for the babies who will be aborted that day, for their parents, and for the people who will perform the abortions.
- Help young women who are pregnant. This help could take various forms: finding a place where they can stay, getting a doctor to care for them, seeking out a program that can help them, gathering clothing for the baby, etc.
- Shiphrah and Puah helped the most vulnerable in society: Hebrew women who were about to give birth. In our case, there are other vulnerable persons, in addition to pregnant women, whom we can help: the unemployed, immigrants, people without a family, people going through financial hardships, etc.
- Raise awareness about changing the "a" word for another "a" word: "adoption" instead of "abortion."

Prayer for unborn babies

Father of goodness,
in your infinite mercy you called us
and gave us the capacity to collaborate with you
to bring new lives into this world.
We pray for those parents who,
making bad use of this capacity
for collaborating with you to form a new life,
destroy it.
We also pray for those who collaborate
in this act of cowardice.
Baby Jesus,
We pray for the babies
who have not been allowed to be born.
We have the certainty that they will enjoy your presence
for all eternity.
Blessed Virgin,
help us to love life from its beginnings
to natural death.
Take care of and protect all mothers who, like you,
bear the gift of life in their wombs.

Amen.

II.
WOMEN WHO CARE FOR THE COMMUNITY

CHAPTER 3

MIRIAM

A good sister and courageous member of the community

Then Jesus said to his disciples, "Whoever wishes to come after me must deny himself, take up his cross, and follow me. For whoever wishes to save his life will lose it, but whoever loses his life for my sake will find it. What profit would there be for one to gain the whole world and forfeit his life? Or what can one give in exchange for his life?"

MATTHEW 16:24–26

Objective

In our twenty-first-century society, communication is instantaneous, time is valuable, and there is a lot to do. And in the confusion that surrounds us, dedicating time and effort to helping others can seem ever more difficult and even outdated.

That is why we will read and delve into the character of Miriam, Moses' sister, who spent her life serving God and the Hebrew people.

Scripture texts: *Exodus 2:4–8; 15:20–21*
Numbers 12:1–15

Introduction to the character

Who was Miriam?

Miriam was Moses' sister. She accompanied him in his work from a young age.

She was attentive to him when his little crib floated down the river, and she told Pharaoh's sister that she knew a woman who could nurse him. Later on, we find her heading up the celebrations of the Hebrew people after they crossed safely through the Red Sea.

Her life unfolded alongside Moses and Aaron, her two brothers, as they guided the people through the desert. And while we know a great deal about Moses' life and activities as the liberator of the Hebrew people, we know little about Miriam and even less about all she did for her community, the Hebrew people. Her testimony as a woman who acted courageously, praised the Lord, and guided the people, and yet who also got angry and irritable, makes her a woman like us. She shows us how wanting to follow and love God is a path to be walked a day at a time, and that the battle to be faithful is not over until our life comes to an end.

Development of the Bible story

Miriam's story begins like many other stories: with the birth of a baby, her brother, Moses, who is born precisely when the Egypt-ian Pharaoh issued a decree stating that all Hebrew boys born in Egypt must be drowned in the river. The mother of Miriam and Moses hides the boy, seeking to deliver him from death at the hands of the Egyptians, but a time comes when it is no longer possible to conceal him. Scripture says Moses' mother places him in a basket, carefully prepared so water will not get in, and leaves him along the banks of the river. It is there that Miriam enters the scene, staying close to the floating crib. When it reaches the hands of the Pharaoh's daughter, who recognizes that the baby is a Hebrew, Miriam suddenly appears and tells her that she knows a Hebrew woman who can nurse the baby:

> So the young woman went and called the child's own mother. Pharaoh's daughter said to her, "Take this child and nurse him for me, and I will pay your wages." So the woman took the child and nursed him. When the child grew, she brought him to Pharaoh's daughter, and he became her son. She named him Moses; for she said, "I drew him out of the water."
>
> Exodus 2:8–10

Thus begins Moses' "bicultural" life. He is raised by his biological mother, with a Hebrew heart, and at the same time, he lives in the royal palace where he has access to Pharaoh's court and an Egyptian education. That is how God prepares Moses for the mission of liberating the Hebrew people from slavery in Egypt.

What courage Miriam shows! What persuasiveness! Pharaoh's daughter did not know where Miriam came from, but in just a few minutes this young Hebrew organized the baby's future and, with it, the future of the Hebrew people, God's people.

With the passage of time, Moses, who was saved from the water by his sister's courage, obtains the Pharaoh's consent for the Hebrew people to leave Egypt and thus be liberated from the oppression under which they lived.

Pharaoh and his servants had a change of heart about the people:

> "What in the world have we done!" they said. "We have released Israel from our service!" So Pharaoh harnessed his chariots and took his army with him. He took six hundred select chariots and all the chariots of Egypt, with officers on all of them. [...] Now Pharaoh was near when the Israelites looked up and saw that the Egyptians had set out after them. Greatly frightened, the Israelites cried out to the LORD. [...] Then the LORD said to Moses: Why are you crying out to me? Tell the Israelites to set out. And you, lift up your staff and stretch out your hand over the sea, and split it in two, that the Israelites may pass through the sea on dry land."
>
> EXODUS 14:5B–7, 10, 15–16

Saved from the Egyptian power, saved from the waters of the sea! The people could only celebrate.

> Then the prophet Miriam, Aaron's sister, took a tambourine in her hand, while all the women went out after her with tambourines, dancing; and she responded to them: Sing to the LORD, for he is gloriously triumphant; horse and chariot he has cast into the sea.
>
> EXODUS 15:20–21

In sacred Scripture, the dance is tied to jubilation and to the adoration of God. Thus, after crossing the Red Sea, the Hebrew people dance. They dance to adore God, to praise him, to thank him, and it is Miriam who guides the people in this celebration. Once again, Miriam is looking out for others, encouraging people to praise God.

They celebrate having been able to regain what belonged to them in the beginning: freedom. That freedom is a gift of God for humanity and which, sadly, other men and women take from us. In the case of the Hebrew people, it was the Egyptians; in our case, it is the terrorists, the drug cartels, the gangs, corrupt governments and more that make us prisoners of fear, insecurity, and uncertainty. But let us be attentive: What should our response be? Should we do nothing while evil expands? Of course not. We have Christ's invitation to be the light of the world and the salt of the earth (Matthew 5:13–14), to fight to change structures, to fight so that good will prevail.

The next time Scripture mentions Miriam is in the Book of Numbers, in chapter twelve. However, things have changed, and now we find her angry and criticizing her brother, Moses, for having married a foreign woman. She is also angry because God speaks only through him:

> Miriam and Aaron spoke against Moses on the pretext of the Cushite woman he had married; for he had in fact married a Cushite woman. They complained, "Is it through Moses alone that the LORD has spoken? Has he not spoken through us also?"
>
> NUMBERS 12:1–2

What are we to make of this? Is Miriam a good or a bad woman? The answer is clear: Miriam is a human being who, like many other human beings, is capable of the most shining devotion and then of being selfish, ungrateful, and envious. That is Miriam, and that is also many of us. We are in a battle to be the best we can be. As Saint Paul tells us in chapter seven of the Letter to the Romans: "We do not do the good we want, but the evil we do not want. We aspire to be generous, to do the right thing all the time, to be detached, to speak well of others, and sometimes we do the wrong thing: We are selfish, critical, gossipy, meddlers, liars, and more."

Giving up on ourselves and others is not the answer; instead, we have to fight to be better. This is a battle we have to fight every day: the battle to be more kind, understanding, and generous, relying always on the help of Christ, who told us before ascending to heaven, "And behold, I am with you always, until the end of the age" (Matthew 28:20b).

What does Miriam teach us?

- To be courageous by defending the lives of children, the unborn, and the homeless. To be attentive to them, taking care of them, helping them to find God, and to be educated in the faith, which means helping them find salvation, just as Miriam did.
- To put the talents and gifts God has given us at the service of others. For some, those gifts will be courage; for others, intelligence, hard work, or the ability to console or give counsel.
- To rejoice at the wonders of the Lord's action in our lives. To rejoice daily, since every day we have reasons to rejoice. Let us not wait for a spectacular event like the crossing of the Red Sea, since perhaps something like that will never happen in our lives. Let us rejoice in our daily lives.
- To make the most of the many occasions we have every day to laugh, rejoice, and thank God.
- To look for God's hand in our lives. To see God guiding, helping, and loving us.
- To praise God's actions and celebrate divine happenings.
- Not to be curious or meddlesome, but to respect others' decisions as long as they do not go against the law, justice, or morality.
- To understand that, in our relationships with our extended family, we are called to live charity and offer them our help.

- To understand that the human person has the potential of acting with great nobility but sometimes fails to do so. But we are called by Christ to be perfect as his heavenly Father is perfect (Matthew 5:48), and we—by the grace of the Lord—must live up to this call.
- To be patient with others, since we generally tend to want others to act according to our expectations. To remember that the most important thing is for them to act in accordance with their condition as sons and daughters of God and human beings.
- To fight to change structures that repress human freedom, structures that do not allow us to live in freedom and truth.

What does the *Catechism of the Catholic Church* tell us?

§1731: "Freedom is the power, rooted in reason and will, to act or not to act, to do this or that, and so to perform deliberate actions on one's own responsibility. By free will one shapes one's own life. Human freedom is a force for growth and maturity in truthand goodness; it attains its perfection when directed toward God, our beatitude."

§1732: Freedom entails the possibility of choosing between good and evil.

§1822: Charity is the theological virtue by which we love God.

§1823: "Jesus makes charity the new commandment (see John 13:34). By loving his own "to the end" (John 13:1), he makes manifest the Father's love which he receives. By loving one another, the disciples imitate the love of Jesus which they themselves receive.

§1826: Charity is superior to all the virtues.

§1829: Living charity produces fruits.

Questions for personal reflection

- Do I remember any of the wonders God has done in my life? Make a list to have them at hand, especially for when you are going through tough times.
- Do I usually thank God for the wonders done in my life? How?
- What gifts or talents has God given me? Am I hard-working, reliable, joyful, a good daughter (son), a good sister (brother), patient, prudent, honest, generous, loyal, etc.?
- Do I put those gifts or talents of God at the service of others? How? What can I do to be more effective in sharing my God-given gifts with others?
- In a moment of prayer, I will think of the names of three people with whom I do not get along well: a member of the family, a member of the community, and a work colleague. Then I will try to answer the following questions about each one of them:
  - Do I know him or her well?
  - Do I know his or her problems?
  - Do I know his or her feelings?
  - What can I do to get along better with him or her?
  - What can I do to help him or her?

Group questions and activities

- Make a list of the different ways the group thinks it would be good to praise God.
- If the group were crossing the Red Sea together with the Hebrew people, what would you feel? What would worry you? What would you do to get to the other shore?
- Share some of the wonders God has done in your life.

- There is a saying: "People are their own worst enemies." What do you think about this statement? Is it true? Give an example demonstrating the truthfulness of this sentence.
- How can we help a person who is going through a hard time, such as any of the problems below?
  - A physical ailment or problem.
  - Financial hardship.
  - A work problem.
  - A legal problem.
  - A family problem or other types of sufferings.
- What can you do for children who have no one to teach them about God?

Practical resolutions

- Don't criticize others. The Letter of Saint James tells us, "For every kind of beast and bird, of reptile and sea creature, can be tamed and has been tamed by the human species, but no human being can tame the tongue" (James 3:7–8).
- Help people who need my help.
- Strive to do the good I want to do.
- Strive not to do the evil I don't want to do.
- Write a letter, an e-mail, or call a friend or family member who lives far away.
- Act on the conclusions I reached in prayer about the three people with whom I do not get along well.
- Remember that my face belongs to others. They are the ones who see me; I do not see myself. Remember to wear a pleasant expression.
- Every night before going to bed, examine my conscience, ask-ing myself, "How did I love God and my fellow brother or sister in Christ today?"

If I speak in human and angelic tongues but do not have love, I am a resounding gong or a clashing cymbal. And if I have the gift of prophecy and comprehend all mysteries and all knowledge; if I have all faith so as to move mountains but do not have love, I am nothing. If I give away everything I own, and if I hand my body over so that I may boast but do not have love, I gain nothing. Love is patient, love is kind. It is not jealous, [love] is not pompous, it is not inflated, it is not rude, it does not seek its own interests, it is not quick-tempered, it does not brood over injury, it does not rejoice over wrongdoing but rejoices with the truth. It bears all things, believes all things, hopes all things, endures all things. Love never fails. [...] So faith, hope, love remain, these three; but the greatest of these is love.

1 Corinthians 13:1-8a, 13

CHAPTER 4

ABIGAIL

A courageous and generous woman

Then the righteous will answer him and say, "Lord, when did we see you hungry and feed you, or thirsty and give you drink? When did we see you a stranger and welcome you, or naked and clothe you? When did we see you ill or in prison, and visit you?" And the king will say to them in reply, "Amen, I say to you, whatever you did for one of these least brothers of mine, you did for me."

MATTHEW 25:37–40

He sat down opposite the treasury and observed how the crowd put money into the treasury. Many rich people put in large sums. A poor widow also came and put in two small coins worth a few cents. Calling his disciples to himself, he said to them, "Amen, I say to you, this poor widow put in more than all the other contributors to the treasury. For they have all contributed from their surplus wealth, but she, from her poverty, has contributed all she had, her whole livelihood."

MARK 12:41–44

Objective

In our days there are women who go against their conscience by following the socially accepted norms. This chapter presents Abigail as an example of a woman who follows her conscience, acting generously and bravely.

Scripture text: *1 Samuel 25:2–42*

Introduction to the character

Who was Abigail?

Abigail was one of King David's wives. Originally she was the wife of Nabal, a rich and ill-tempered man. When Nabal refused to give food to David—the future king—and to his soldiers, who had previously taken care of Nabal's shepherds, David decided to take revenge and headed over to Nabal's farm to kill Nabal and his men.

Abigail took matters into her own hands, secretly preparing a huge amount of food and bringing it to David. When she met him on the way, she thanked him for having taken care of the shepherds and asked pardon for her husband's attitude.

Shortly afterward, Nabal died, and Abigail married David.

Development of the Bible story

First Samuel recounts the story of Abigail's courage and generosity. It tells us about a man named Nabal, who is quite important and wealthy, since he has three thousand sheep and a thousand goats. Nabal is at his farm in Carmel because he is shearing his sheep.

Nabal's wife, Abigail, is intelligent and beautiful, while Scripture tells us that Nabal is harsh and bad-mannered. What a match!

While Nabal is home shearing his sheep, David and his men are out in the desert without much food or drink left to go around. David sends some of his men to Nabal's farm with the order to greet him and tell him:

> "I have just heard that shearers are with you. Now, when your shepherds were with us, we did them no injury, neither did they miss anything while they were in Carmel. Ask your servants and they will tell you. Look kindly on these young men, since we come at a festival time. Please give your servants and your son David whatever you can."
>
> 1 Samuel 25:7–8

Nabal's answer is a resounding "no." He says he won't give him any of his bread, wine, or the meat of the animals that he sacrificed in order to feed David and his people. David's young men return and give him Nabal's answer. Without missing a beat, David says, "Let everyone strap on his sword" (1 Samuel 25:13).

Now the war is really on. David takes 400 armed men with him to where Nabal is. This is where Abigail enters the picture. One of her servants tells her about what has happened and how David and his men had always acted rightly by Nabal's men, meaning that they never mistreated them, and how Nabal's shepherds never lacked for anything while they were among David's men.

The injustices of evil men! But what could be expected of Nabal, whose own servant says of him, "He is such a scoundrel that no one can talk to him" (1 Samuel 25:17)?

The text continues, telling us how Abigail takes two hundred loaves, two skins of wine, five dressed sheep, roasted grain, a hundred cakes of pressed raisins, and 200 cakes of pressed figs, and loads them onto donkeys. And without saying a word to her husband, she sets out in search of David.

Meanwhile, David and his men are on their way to Nabal.

"David had just been saying: 'Indeed, it was in vain that I guarded all this man's possessions in the wilderness, so that nothing of his was missing. He has repaid good with evil. May God do thus to David, and more, if by morning I leave a single male alive among all those who belong to him'" (1 Samuel 25:21–22).

Abigail intercepts David and, getting off the donkey, prostrates herself before him with her face to the ground, saying:

> "Listen to the words of your maidservant. My lord, do not pay any attention to that scoundrel Nabal, for he is just like his name. His name means fool, and he acts the fool. I, your maidservant, did not see the young men whom my lord sent. Now, therefore, my lord, as the LORD lives, and as you live, the LORD has kept you from shedding blood and from avenging yourself by your own hand. [...] Accept this gift, then, which your maidservant has brought for my lord, and let it be given to the young men who follow my lord."
>
> 1 SAMUEL 25:24–27

I had good reason to title this chapter "Abigail: A courageous and generous woman," since she reacts quickly to the needs of others, forgetting herself. She responds energetically to the injustice committed by her husband, extending her hand to the needy.

David's response to Abigail is a masterpiece:

> "Blessed is the LORD, the God of Israel, who sent you to meet me today. Blessed is your good judgment and blessed are you yourself. Today you have prevented me from shedding blood and rescuing myself with my own hand. Otherwise, as the LORD, the God of Israel, lives, who has kept me from harming you, if you had not come so promptly to meet me, by dawn Nabal would not have had so much as one male left alive." David then took from

her what she had brought him and said to her: "Go to your home in peace! See, I have listened to your appeal and have granted your request."

1 SAMUEL 25:32–35

David calls her a woman of good judgment, congratulates her for her swift action, blesses her for her intervention, and assures her that she can count on him. What a change from the man who had been ready to annihilate Nabal! Now he cannot stop blessing the Lord and Abigail! Thus was Saint Francis de Sales' saying fulfilled: "You will catch more flies with a spoonful of honey than with a hundred barrels of vinegar."

The story continues with Abigail's return home, where she finds Nabal completely drunk as he is celebrating a banquet. The next day, once he is sober, she tells him what happened. The Lord strikes Nabal with a heart attack, and he is paralyzed and then dies a few days later.

When David finds out Nabal has died, he says, "Blessed be the LORD, who has defended my cause against the insult from Nabal, and who restrained his servant from doing evil, but has repaid Nabal for his evil deeds" (1 Samuel 25:39). Then he sends a marriage proposal to Abigail, who accepts and becomes his wife. It is worth noting that she is one of many wives of David. Let us recall that Christian morality did not come to the Hebrew people until the arrival of Jesus.

What does Abigail teach us?

- Not to get discouraged if we act badly, but to be quick to repent, quick to apologize, and quick to move on.
- That when someone offends us, Iremember it is better to be offended than to be the one who offends. That's choosing the lesser of two evils.
- To understand that revenge is not a solution, since it only worsens the offense. How paradoxical is David's attitude: After being offended, he decides to commit a greater offense.
- To catch a glimpse of how far an act of generosity can go.
- To understand that generosity is a virtue that makes us better human beings, better imitators of Christ, who, while hanging on the cross and seeing his Mother and the disciple whom he loved, said to his mother, "Woman, behold your son" and then told the disciple, "Behold your mother" (John 19:26–27).
- To look out for the good of others, since the more we give, the more we are enriched.
- To defend the most needy, those who have no one to defend them. Jesus tells us, "Amen, I say to you, whatever you did for one of these least brothers of mine, you did for me" (Matthew 25:40).
- To fight injustice.
- To be attentive to others' needs and to go ahead and meet them, like the Virgin Mary at the wedding of Cana when she told Jesus, "They have no [more] wine" (John 2:3).
- To know that to work for justice, we must do so with charity.
- Never to refuse to give food to the hungry.
- To react quickly, like Abigail, when someone has a need.

What does the *Catechism of the Catholic Church* tell us?

§1776: Humans have in their "hearts a law inscribed by God." The human conscience is humanity's "most secret core and sanctuary" where one is "alone with God whose voice echoes" in the depths of each human heart (*GS* 16).

§221: God is love.

§221: God's love is everlasting.

§1832: Generosity is a fruit of the Holy Spirit.

§1756: One may not do evil so that good may result from it.

§1795: The conscience is man's most sacred core.

§1798: A well-formed conscience is upright and truthful.

Questions for personal reflection

- Have I ever run into people like Nabal, people who think only of themselves and who care nothing for others, people who do whatever it takes to look good, to get more for themselves, to be well-liked, to have a better reputation? Have I acted this way with others?
- Jesus said, "A good person out of the store of goodness in his heart produces good, but an evil person out of a store of evil produces evil; for from the fullness of the heart the mouth speaks" (Luke 6:45). What is my heart full of? What do I talk about? My words speak for me: What do they say?
- When someone does or says things that seem wrong to me, like what Nabal said to David, how do I react? Do I get angry to such an extent that, like David, I want to take revenge? Do I measure the consequences and possible outcomes of my actions? Do I realice that I am going to act just as wrongly as the other person?

- Abigail proved herself to be a brave and generous woman. Am I brave, or do I let the days and months go by as I avoid facing a problem? What can I do to be courageous when the moment requires it? What can I do to have feelings of generosity in my heart, like Abigail?
- How do I treat those who are in touch with me: family, friends, colleagues, community, etc.? With Abigail's goodness or with Nabal's coldness and selfishness? What can I do to treat them better?
- Why did David ask Abigail to marry him? What did he see in her that caught his eye so much?
- It is a reality that we are not all equal. We do not think the same way, nor do we like the same things, nor do we react the same way. Thus it is natural that there will be differences among us. With whom do I have my differences? Are they big or little? What can I do to smooth them over?

Group questions and activities

- In the following passages, compare David's words with Nabal's.
  - What do each person's words tells us about what sort of people he is?
  - Which of them would I prefer to have as a friend? Why?
  - Do I know anyone who is like David? Like Nabal?

David

"Say to him, 'Peace be with you, my brother, and with your family, and with all who belong to you. I have just heard that shearers are with you. Now, when your shepherds were with us, we did them no injury, neither did they miss anything while they were in Carmel. Ask your servants and they will tell you. Look kindly on these young men, since we come at a festival time. Please give your servants and your son David whatever you can.'"

1 SAMUEL 25:6–8

Nabal

> But Nabal answered the servants of David: "Who is David? Who is the son of Jesse? Nowadays there are many servants who run away from their masters. Must I take my bread, my wine, my meat that I have slaughtered for my own shearers, and give them to men who come from who knows where?"
>
> 1 SAMUEL 25:10–11

- In life, we face hard times and *very* hard times, both for us and for others. During those times, a consoling truth can help us: God is our Father who loves us and does not forget us. The words of the prophet Isaiah remind us, "Can a mother forget her infant, be without tenderness for the child of her womb? Even should she forget, I will never forget you" (Isaiah 49:15).
  - Do these words mean something to us?
  - Do they help us?
  - Write a motto that will help you live in the peace of knowing that you are God's child.
- Abigail served as a mediator between two men who had their differences, and with her gentleness and generosity, was able to achieve peace.
  - Conduct an "interview" with Abigail, analyzing what she was thinking, what motivated her to act as she did, whether she was scared, etc.
- Reflect on the Gospel of Matthew:

> "You have heard that it was said, 'You shall love your neighbor and hate your enemy.' But I say to you, love your enemies, and pray for those who persecute you, that you may be children of your heavenly Father, for he makes his sun rise on the bad and the good, and causes rain to

fall on the just and the unjust. For if you love those who love you, what recompense will you have? Do not the tax collectors do the same? And if you greet your brothers only, what is unusual about that? Do not the pagans do the same? So be perfect, just as your heavenly Father is perfect."

MATTHEW 5:43–48

▷ What is the message of this passage for us?

Practical resolutions

- Daily I will offer God my sorrows and joys, discouragement and enthusiasm, hard work and tiredness.
- There are moments in life when our first reaction will be anger and selfishness. I will make those moments just that—moments—and not my ordinary way of behaving.
- I will make an extra effort daily to give myself to others.
- I will participate actively and enthusiastically in activities that combat hunger in my city.
- I will motivate myself and those around me to live the virtue of generosity.
- I will seek out people, places, and situations where I can put this virtue into practice.
- I will forget the small disagreements that come up daily.
- I will take others' needs seriously. Like Abigail, I will reach out to those most in need.
- I will help organize and promote events in my parish. Like Abigail, I will forget myself so as to give to others.
- I won't give up in times of tension and difficulty.

Prayer

Take, Lord, and receive

Take, Lord, and receive all my liberty,
my memory, my understanding
and my entire will,
All I have and call my own.

You have given all to me.
To you, Lord, I return it.

Everything is yours; do with it what you will.
Give me only your love and your grace.
That is enough for me.

SAINT IGNATIUS OF LOYOLA

III.
USED, ABUSED, AND ANGRY WOMEN

CHAPTER 5

HAGAR

A woman who was used and expelled

God takes care of all people:

> *Thus says the* Lord*: In a time of favor I answer you, on the day of salvation I help you. […] Along the roadways they shall find pasture, on every barren height shall their pastures be. They shall not hunger or thirst; nor shall scorching wind or sun strike them; for he who pities them leads them and guides them beside springs of water. I will turn all my mountains into roadway, and make my highways level.*
>
> Isaiah 49:8–11

Objective

We live in a world where some women are used and abused. This chapter will show how God cared for Hagar, even when the social structures had sent her away with her son. It will also encourage us to abandon ourselves into God's hands.

Scripture text: *Genesis 16:1–16 and 21:9–21*

Introduction to the characters

Who was Hagar?

Hagar was an Egyptian woman, the slave of Sarai, the wife of Abram, who found himself in a difficult situation when his wife, Sarai, could not have children.

As a solution to the infertility problem, Sarai proposed that Abram sleep with the slave, Hagar, so that he could have a child. When Hagar got pregnant, she began to look down on her mistress Sarai, who abused Hagar so much that she fled into the desert.

And it was in this desert that the angel of the Lord found her, comforted her, and encouraged her to return to the camp, where she gave birth to Ishmael.

In time, Sarai finally gave Abram a son and asked him to dismiss Hagar. Hagar had nowhere else to go but into the desert with her son, and once more the angel of God intervened to save them both.

Hagar: a woman who was used and abused, but rescued by God.

Of course, this is a story with dramatic elements: sexual relations, abuse and jealousy, abandonment and protection.

Like any good story, it begins with a solemn affirmation: "Abram's wife Sarai had borne him no children" (Genesis 16:1). And from this statement the rest of the story unfolds, involving Sarai, her husband, Abram; her slave, Hagar; and the angel of the Lord.

To be able to understand this story, we have to go back to that time and understand that the way of thinking and acting and the principles that governed the lives of these people were very different from those that govern today's world. We live in a world that has already known Christ and that is governed by the commandment he left us to love God and our neighbor as we love ourselves.

At that time, it was not so. Thus the first thing we notice is that Sarai has a slave named Hagar. For us, slavery is something unjust and vile, but at that time it was a common practice, and we see it in various Bible passages.

We also notice that Sarai tells Abram, "The LORD has kept me from bearing children. Have intercourse with my maid; perhaps I will have sons through her" (Genesis 16:2). How could a son born from Abram's union with Hagar become Sarai's son? To understand this, we have to see how slavery was understood at that time. The slave was the master's total possession. Her body belonged to the master, so her son did as well. This is strange for us, citizens of the twenty-first century.

Abram obeys his wife, sleeps with Hagar and gets her pregnant. Upon realizing that she has Abram's son in her womb, Hagar begins to look down upon her mistress. Immediately Sarai tells Abram, "I myself gave my maid to your embrace; but ever since she knew she was pregnant, I have lost stature in her eyes." Abram answers her, "Your maid is in your power.

Do to her what you regard as right" (Genesis 16:5–6). "*She is your slave. Do to her what you think is best.*" What harsh words! How can he say, "*Do to her what you think is best*" as if she were some kind of an object? Poor Hagar. They used and abused her.

And since Sarai mistreats her, Hagar flees. Scripture tells us that the Lord's angel finds her in the desert next to a spring and asks her:

> "Hagar, maid of Sarai, where have you come from and where are you going?" She answered, "I am running away from my mistress, Sarai." But the LORD's angel told her: "Go back to your mistress and submit to her authority. I will make your descendants so numerous," added the LORD's angel, "that they will be too many to count. [...] You are now pregnant and shall bear a son; you shall name him Ishmael, for the LORD has heeded your affliction."
>
> GENESIS 16:8–11

Hagar gives birth to a boy, and Abram names him Ishmael.

The reader will note how, from this point forward, Sarai's name changes to Sarah and Abram's to Abraham. This is because in the mentality of that time, a name change meant a change in destiny. Chapter seventeen of Genesis tells how God changed Sarai's and Abram's names, since their lives would have a new destiny following Isaac's birth.

Time passes, Isaac grows, and the day comes when they celebrate his weaning with a banquet. This is another custom that is totally unfamiliar to the men and women of our times. Children are eventually weaned, but the event is not celebrated with a banquet.

It is at this banquet that Sarah spots Hagar's son playing with her son, Isaac, and she tells Abraham, "Drive out that slave and her son! No son of that slave is going to share the inheritance with my son Isaac!" (Genesis 21:10).

Abraham is distressed because Ishmael is also his son. God calms his heart, telling him that the son of the slave woman will one day become a great nation, since he is also his descendant. Genesis tells us that:

> Early the next morning Abraham got some bread and a skin of water and gave them to Hagar. Then, placing the child on her back, he sent her away. As she roamed aimlessly in the wilderness of Beer-sheba, the water in the skin was used up. So she put the child down under one of the bushes, and then went and sat down opposite him, about a bowshot away; for she said to herself, "I cannot watch the child die."
>
> GENESIS 21:14–16

God hears the child's cries and the Lord's angel comes down from heaven to tell Hagar:

> "What is the matter, Hagar? Do not fear; God has heard the boy's voice. [...] Get up, lift up the boy and hold him by the hand; for I will make of him a great nation." Then God opened her eyes, and she saw a well of water. She went and filled the skin with water, and then let the boy drink.
>
> GENESIS 21:17–19

The Scripture text continues, telling us how God takes care of Ishmael, who grows up and lives in the desert, marrying an Egyptian woman.

What a story! Hagar was used and abused! Her situation of enslavement made her a perfect target, since the law did not grant her any rights. When Sarai needed her, she used her, and when she got in the way, she threw her out. But God, who is ever faithful, always looked out for her.

What does Hagar teach us?

- That God is always attentive to his creatures, no matter who they are or what situation they are in.
- Not to let ourselves be carried away by desperation and sadness.
- To be at peace, knowing that God acts in our lives and in the lives of all human beings.
- To trust in divine providence, which is the care that God takes of his creatures.
- That God prefers the humble, and this confounds the powerful who are used to being the center of attention. The Gospel of Matthew tells us about this: "I give praise to you, Father, Lord of heaven and earth, for although you have hidden these things from the wise and the learned you have revealed them to the childlike. Yes, Father, such has been your gracious will" (Matthew 11:25–26).
- That the final victory does not come from man's power but from God. As the Book of Revelation tells us, "Now have salvation and power come, and the kingdom of our God and the authority of his Anointed. [...] They conquered him by the blood of the Lamb and by the word of their testimony. [...] Therefore, rejoice, you heavens, and you who dwell in them" (Revelation 12:10–12a).
- That God is the Lord of history.
- That God is always faithful.
- That when things go badly and it seems there is no way out, God hears our pleas, just as he heard the baby boy's cries. And he tells us, as he told Hagar, "What is the matter...? Do not fear; God has heard the [...] voice in this plight of his" (Genesis 21:17).
- To be ready to help and defend those most abandoned by society, including widows, orphans, immigrants, addicts, etc.

- That there is always a future, that we must not stay stuck in the here and now, but look to the future with hope. Likewise, God did not abandon Hagar but promised her, "I will make your descendants so numerous...they will be too many to count" (Genesis 16:10).

What does the *Catechism of the Catholic Church* tell us?

§302: "Creation has its own goodness and proper perfection, but it did not spring forth complete from the hands of the Creator. The universe was created 'in a state of journeying' (*in statu viae*) toward an ultimate perfection yet to be attained, to which God has destined it."

§303: Divine providence is concrete and immediate.

§304: God's has primacy and absolute lordship over history and the world.

§306: God makes use of his creatures.

§307: God also makes use of his creatures' cooperation.

§322: Christ invites us to trust in the providence of God.

§2539: Envy refers to sadness at the sight of another's goods.

Questions for personal reflection

- In times of trial, do I do anything to increase my faith?
- How do I react when trials and pain come into my life? Do I get angry at God? Do I ignore God? Do I come closer to the Lord? Do I blame God?
- Do I get discouraged easily? What do I do when I feel sad? What do I stop doing?
- Have I ever been in an emotional desert where I thought no one understood me? Did I feel alone even though I was surrounded by other people? How did I react?

- Have I sent any member of my family or my community to the desert? That is, have I distanced them from my friendship, company, affection, and understanding? Why? Do I think I was right to do so? What will I do to remedy it?
- How do I see and relate to God? Do I love the Lord?
- Am I convinced that all the efforts I make to be faithful to God have great value for eternity?
- What are the different ways God has shown me his help, company, and care in moments of my life when I felt sad, alone, overwhelmed, or worried?

Group questions and activities

- Reflect on the following verse from the Book of Judith:

  So while we wait for the salvation that comes from him,
  let us call upon him to help us, and he will hear our cry
  if it pleases him.

  Judith 8:17

  - Each member of the group will write a sentence expressing her feelings about how God has acted in her life.
  - The group members will compare what they wrote.

- Today there are women in the world who find themselves in a situation similar to Hagar's. They are not slaves, but they are being exploited, mistreated, used, and abused, and no one is taking care of them.
  - Give examples of women who are in this situation.
  - Reflect on how we could help them.
  - Remember that God hears their cry and acts to help them through other human beings.

- Why do you think Hagar began to mock Sarai after realizing she was pregnant?
  - Give examples of situations where a person with advantages mocks the disadvantaged.
  - How did Sarai treat Hagar after being mocked by her?
  - What do we learn from this situation?
- Brainstorm ideas about the feelings this passage stirs up:

  God heard the boy's voice, and God's angel called to Hagar from heaven: "What is the matter, Hagar? Do not fear; God has heard the boy's voice in this plight of his. Get up, lift up the boy and hold him by the hand; for I will make of him a great nation." Then God opened her eyes, and she saw a well of water. She went and filled the skin with water, and then let the boy drink.

  GENESIS 21:17-19

- Read the following psalm:

  I say to the LORD: You are my God;
  listen, LORD, to the words of my pleas.
  LORD, my master, my strong deliverer,
  you cover my head on the day of armed conflict.
  For I know the LORD will take up the cause of the needy,
  justice for the poor.
  Then the righteous will give thanks to your name;
  the upright will dwell in your presence.

  PSALM 140:7–8, 13–14

  - It can be hard to understand this psalm in a world where it seems that just the opposite happens. It seems that "he who compromises gets ahead," the bully gets his way, and the underdog gets trampled.
  - Discuss two phrases from this psalm: "Lord...my strong deliverer" and "I know the Lord will...[bring] justice for the poor."

Practical resolutions

- I will ask God to open my eyes as he opened Hagar's eyes: "Then God opened her eyes, and she saw a well of water. She went and filled the skin with water, and then let the boy drink" (Genesis 21:19). God is there for me to come to him, to be my "well" where I can draw water, especially in hard times.
- I will understand that God has his moments that are very different from ours. Just as the prophet Habakkuk said, "If it delays, wait for it, it will surely come, it will not be late" (Habakkuk 2:3).
- In difficult moments, I will remember that Jesus said, "Come to me, all you who labor and are burdened, and I will give you rest" (Matthew 11:28).
- I will look for information about the message Saint Faustina Kowalska received from Jesus when he asked her to tell the world about God's infinite mercy.
- I will tell all my relatives and friends what I learned about the message of divine mercy.
- I will pray the Divine Mercy chaplet every day with infinite trust in God's mercy.

Divine Mercy chaplet

To be prayed daily, preferably at 3 o'clock in the afternoon, the hour when Jesus died for us (using a rosary is recommended).

- In the name of the Father, and of the Son, and of the Holy Spirit.
- Our Father.
- Hail Mary.
- Creed.
- On the large bead, say this prayer before each decade:

  Eternal Father, I offer You
the Body and Blood, Soul and Divinity
of Your dearly beloved Son, Our Lord Jesus Christ,
in atonement for our sins
and those of the whole world.

- On the ten little beads of each decade:

  For the sake of His sorrowful Passion,
have mercy on us
and on the whole world.

- At the end, after praying the five decades, say three times:

  Holy God,
Holy Mighty One,
Holy Immortal One,
have mercy on us
and on the whole world.

CHAPTER 6

LEAH

A woman pushed aside by those who should have cared for her

God chose the foolish of the world to shame the wise, and God chose the weak of the world to shame the strong, and God chose the lowly and despised of the world, those who count for nothing, to reduce to nothing those who are something, so that no human being might boast before God. As it is written, "Whoever boasts, should boast in the Lord."*

1 CORINTHIANS 1:27-29, 31

There is no creature so small and worthless that it does not show forth the goodness of God.

IMITATION OF CHRIST, II, 4,2

Objective

We live in a society where decisions are often made in a utilitarian way: If it serves my interests, good; if not, I drop it. If I like it, I go ahead. If I don't like it, then *adiós*. If it looks good to me, I'm in. If it doesn't look like a winner, I'm out.

In spite of having been pushed aside by her father, husband, and sister, Leah plays a very important role in salvation history and teaches us to trust that God brings good things out of what, in human eyes, appears to be nothing more than a disgrace.

Scripture texts: *Genesis 29:1–30*
Genesis 35:23–26
Genesis 49:8–12
Genesis 49:29–31

Introduction to the character

Who was Leah?

Leah was the first wife of Jacob and the mother of six of his sons: Reuben, Simeon, Levi, Judah, Issachar, and Zebulun; she was also the mother of his daughter, Dinah.

Leah's story is an unprecedented one. Her sister, Rachel, was given in marriage to Jacob. Yet, at the hour when the wedding was to be celebrated, her father, Laban, took Leah to Jacob in her full wedding attire, which included a veil that covered her face, and he slept with her.

The next day, when Jacob realized that he had been swindled, he angrily confronted Laban and demanded that he give him Rachel, whom he loved, and not Leah, who "had dull eyes."

This is how the story of these sisters unfolds. Both were Jacob's wives, although he clearly preferred Rachel. Hence the subtitle of this chapter: "a woman pushed aside by those who should have" loved and protected her: her father and her husband.

The extraordinary thing about this story is that the line of descent leading to Jesus came from Leah, not from Rachel. Through Leah, considered the "loser" according to human standards, came salvation!

Development of the Bible story

This Bible story begins with Isaac, the son of Abraham and Sarah, who calls his son Jacob to bless him and tell him:

> "You shall not marry a Canaanite woman! Go now to Paddan-aram, to the home of your mother's father Bethuel, and there choose a wife for yourself from among the daughters of Laban, your mother's brother. May God Almighty bless you and make you fertile, multiply you that you may become an assembly of peoples. May God extend to you and your descendants the blessing of Abraham, so that you may gain possession of the land where you are residing, which he assigned to Abraham."
>
> GENESIS 28:1–4

Jacob sets out in obedience to his father, leaving Beer-sheba and heading toward Haran.

> Looking about, he saw a well in the open country, with three flocks of sheep huddled near it, for flocks were watered from that well. [...] Jacob said to [the shepherds], "My brothers, where are you from?" "We are from Haran," they replied. Then he asked them, "Do you know Laban, son of Nahor?" "We do," they answered. He inquired further, "Is he well?" "He is," they answered; "and here comes his daughter Rachel with the sheep."
>
> GENESIS 29:2, 4–6

Jacob introduces himself to Rachel as the son of Rebekah, her father's relative. Excited, she runs to tell her father that his sister's son has come. Happy to welcome his nephew, Laban embraces him and brings him into his home, where he stays for a month.

The Bible story continues, telling us that Laban had two daughters: the elder was named Leah and the younger was named Rachel. "Leah had dull eyes, but Rachel was shapely and beautiful" (Genesis 29:17). The story of these two sisters has been repeated in many families throughout human history: one daughter is beautiful and the other is not; one son is an excellent athlete, while the other is clumsy. Such is life.

Now the question arises: what does it mean that Leah had "dull eyes?" For us modern readers, hearing that someone lacks shiny eyes doesn't mean much. Perhaps we would have said, "Well, let her use eye drops to put some moisture in her eyes." To get a better understanding of what it meant, we have to go back to the original language in which the Book of Genesis was written, which is Hebrew.

It is difficult to know exactly what the phrase "she had dull eyes" meant in Leah's day. There are different interpretations in the various Bible translations. One says that "Leah had dull eyes," another says she had "weak" eyes, and another says "she had soft eyes." Although we cannot know exactly what happened to Leah, we do know that she had some kind of a problem with her eyes, and that, compared to her sister Rachel—whom the text tells us was shapely and beautiful—Leah was on the "losing" side when it came to looks.

The romantic part of the story begins with the succinct phrase, "Jacob loved Rachel" (Genesis 29:18). He goes to his Uncle Laban and tells him, "I will serve you seven years for your younger daughter" (Genesis 29:18). Laban accepts the proposal, since he would rather give his daughter to his nephew than to another man. It is worth clarifying that in antiquity there was no awareness of the genetic problems that could come from a marriage between close relatives. At that time, marrying a cousin was not unusual, and it was even seen as a normal way to preserve one's own race.

Jacob works the seven years he agreed upon with Laban in order to obtain Rachel in marriage. This is another custom that no longer exists in today's world. The scriptural text tells us that those years "seemed to him like a few days because of his love for her" (Genesis 29:20). Now that *is* romantic.

Once he has served his time, Jacob tells Laban that he upheld his end of the deal and that he must give him his wife. And this is where the problems begin. The text tells us that:

> Laban invited all the local inhabitants and gave a banquet. At nightfall he took his daughter Leah and brought her to Jacob, and he consummated the marriage with her. [...] In the morning, there was Leah! So Jacob said to Laban: "How could you do this to me! Was it not for Rachel that I served you? Why did you deceive me?" Laban replied, "It is not the custom in our country to give the younger daughter before the firstborn. Finish the bridal week for this one, and then the other will also be given to you in return for another seven years of service with me."
>
> GENESIS 29:22–27

Now Laban had really fooled Jacob, giving him one daughter for the other, the "weak-eyed" daughter instead of the stunning beauty. You will rightly say, "Well, didn't Jacob notice?" Experts in the customs of that time say that bridal dresses were made with a great deal of fabric and that it was common to have the face covered with a veil.

Jacob accepts the deal. After the nuptial week with Leah—that was how long wedding feasts lasted—Laban hands over his daughter Rachel. Now we have to assume that Jacob took a good look at the woman he was marrying! The Bible tells us, "Jacob then consummated his marriage with Rachel also, and he loved her more than Leah. Thus he served Laban another seven years" (Genesis 29:30).

Poor Leah went from bad to worse. First her father tricked a man into marrying her. What great sorrow to know that Jacob married her because of a deception. And now it turned out that Jacob was wildly in love with her sister, Rachel, whom he loved more than her. It is that constant competition between two women for a man's love,and the man's constant preference for the pretty woman.

Life at Jacob's house continues. We know by the Scripture text that he had relations with Leah and with Rachel, and with the maidservants of each one of them. From these sexual relations, twelve children were born, the heads of the twelve tribes of Israel.

But how life surprises us. Leah, the "Ugly Betty," the woman with "weak eyes," the one who was not Jacob's great love, the one who took second place to Rachel in Jacob's affections, and by all accounts the "loser" of the story, was the one from whom Judah was born, and through Judah, Jesus the Savior. The beginning of the Gospel of Matthew tells us:

> Abraham became the father of Isaac, Isaac the father of Jacob, Jacob the father of Judah and his brothers. Judah became the father of Perez and Zerah. [...] Salmon was the father of Boaz, whose mother was Rahab. Boaz became the father of Obed, whose mother was Ruth. Obed became the father of Jesse, Jesse the father of David the king. [...] Eliud was the father of Eleazar. Eleazar became the father of Matthan, Matthan the father of Jacob, Jacob the father of Joseph, the husband of Mary. Of her was born Jesus who is called the Messiah.
>
> MATTHEW 1:2–3, 5–6, 15–16

What an honor, to be the great-great-great-great grandmother of Jesus!

The story of Leah's life ends when she is buried in the cave of Machpelah, in the land of Canaan, in the field that Abraham had bought to bury his wife Sarah and where he was also buried, along with his son Isaac and his wife Rebekah, and Jacob and our beloved Leah (Genesis 49:29–32), while Rachel was buried outside of Bethlehem.

This was another honor conferred on Leah, that of being buried with the patriarchs of the Hebrew people.

Take note: Leah the "loser" turned out to be Leah the winner. This teaches us that human values are different from the values of God. What is golden in human eyes are not so in God's eyes. That is, what we consider valuable—beauty, fame, money, power, race, etc.—is not important to God. For God, what matters is the heart.

"A clean heart create for me, God" (Psalm 51:12).

What does Leah teach us?

- Not to worry so much about what others think. Not to let ourselves be led by their hierarchy of values.
- To ask ourselves, "What does God want from me?" and to put that first.
- Not to be discouraged if we do not meet the expectations that others have for us.
- To understand that physical beauty is not everything.
- To see others as God sees them.
- Not to envy those who have more than me. Not just money, but also beauty, power, family, knowledge, contacts, affection, wisdom, etc.
- To remember what the Tenth Commandment tells us: "You shall not covet your neighbor's goods."
- To aspire to be the person God wants me to be, regardless of whether I have a lot or a little. I am a child of God, and I am called to give the best of myself.

- To always keep in mind Jesus' commandment in the Gospel of Matthew: "Be perfect, just as your heavenly Father is perfect" (Matthew 5:48). Notice that the Gospel uses God's perfection rather than human as a reference point.
- To remember that God created humanity, and God does not make mistakes. "Then God said: Let us make human beings in our image, after our likeness" (Genesis 1:26).
- To remember that God made all of us in his own image and likeness, so no human being is worth less than another.
- To treat others with charity, regardless of their race, color, civil status, culture, etc.
- To see the face of God in others.
- To remember that each of us will have to render an account to God for our actions, so I should worry about what I will give God, without meddling in others' lives.
- To remember that if I am going to intervene in others' lives, it is to help, not to criticize.

What does the *Catechism of the Catholic Church* tell us?

§1935: Human equality "rests essentially on...dignity as persons and the rights that flow from it. Every form of social or cultural discrimination in fundamental personal rights on the grounds of sex, race, color, social conditions, language, or religion must be curbed and eradicated as incompatible with God's design" (*GS* 29.2).

§364: Concerning the dignity of the human body for all humanity is made in the image and likeness of the invisible God

§374: The first man was not only created good, but was also established in friendship with his Creator.

§396: All humanity is "dependent on [the] Creator, and subject to the laws of creation and to the moral norms that govern the use of freedom."

§1936: Human beings need others, as their giftedness is not distributed equally.

§1711: "Endowed with a spiritual soul, with intellect and with free will, the human person is from his very conception ordered to God."

Questions for personal reflection

- Have I tricked anyone like Laban did? Not by marrying one daughter off in place of another, but by saying or doing something other than what I had originally agreed upon?
- Can I make up for the wrong I did in some way?
- Do I judge people by their physical appearance, material possessions, by my good chemistry with them?
- Do I have the tendency to look down on those whom I consider "inferior" or "different?"
- Do I tend to help, to be more caring and courteous with people I consider "inferior" or "different?"
- Have I felt I am not loved by those who should love me (husband, parents, children, siblings, etc.)? What do I feel? What am I doing about it?
- Leah is remembered more for not receiving her husband's love than for being Judah's mother. Do I remember others by their good points or by their bad points?
- Do I think my life is different or better because I believe, love, and hope in God? Does having God in my life fill me with happiness and peace?

Group questions and activities

- Number 1936 of the *Catechism of the Catholic Church* states that on coming into the world, humans are not equipped with everything they need for developing their bodily and spiritual life. We need others. The catechism says:

  Differences appear tied to age, physical abilities, intellectual or moral aptitudes, the benefits derived from social commerce, and the distribution of wealth (*GS* 29.2). The "talents" are not distributed equally (see Matthew 25:14–31, Luke 19:11–27).

  Reflect together on this statement, answer the following questions, and give examples:

  - What does the catechism mean by "physical abilities?"
  - What does the catechism mean by "intellectual aptitudes?"
  - What does the catechism mean by "moral aptitudes?"
  - What does the catechism mean by "the benefits derived from social commerce?"

- Reflect together on this statement: In number 1936, the *Catechism of the Catholic Church* states that these differences—physical abilities, intellectual or moral aptitudes, etc.—are part of the plan of God, who wants us to receive what we need from others. But further on it says something very important: that those who possess particular capacities are to share them with others so that we enrich one another.
- What does it mean that each one is to receive what he needs from others?
- What does it mean to say that those with particular capacities are to share them with others so as to enrich one another?

- Genesis says:

  Then God said: Let us make human beings in our image, after our likeness. [...] God created mankind in his image; in the image of God he created them; male and female he created them. God blessed them and God said to them: Be fertile and multiply; fill the earth and subdue it. And so it happened. God looked at everything he had made, and found it very good.

  GENESIS 1:26–27, 30–31

  Reflect together on this statement.

  - What does it mean that humanity is created in God's image and likeness?
  - What does it mean that God looked at everything he had made (including human beings) and found it very good?
  - Read and reflect on the parable of the talents in the Gospel of Matthew 25:14–30. Go back to the first question in this exercise and relate them.
  - What does it mean that the Lord will ask us to render an account for the talents given to us?
  - Why does the Lord get irritated or rejoice?

Practical resolutions

- Not to judge a person by what I see on the outside. As the saying goes, "Appearances are deceiving."
- To value people simply because they are creatures of God, regardless of the place they occupy on earth, their qualities, or their defects.
- To rejoice with others' joys and grieve with them over their sorrows. To accompany them on their path through life.

- In our times, there are men and women who love others instead of their husband or wife, and by "others" I am referring not just to another person, but also to sports on television, friends, soap operas, work, etc. If I know someone in this situation, I will pray for him or her and not judge.
- To make an effort to see the positive side of people.
- To help someone who needs my help. Not to make excuses like "we don't get along" or "she gave me a dirty look" or "he was rude to me ten years ago," etc. If he or she needs my help, I will give it. End of discussion.

Prayer

Lord, I believe in you: increase my faith.
I trust in you: strengthen my trust.
I love you: let me love you more and more.
I am sorry for my sins: deepen my sorrow.

I worship you as my first beginning,
I long for you as my last end,
I praise you as my constant helper,
And call on you as my loving protector.

Guide me by your wisdom,
Correct me with your justice,
Comfort me with your mercy,
Protect me with your power.

I offer you, Lord, my thoughts: to be fixed on you;
My words: to have you for their theme;
My actions: to reflect my love for you;
My sufferings: to be endured for your greater glory.

I want to do what you ask of me:
In the way you ask,
For as long as you ask,
Because you ask it.

Lord, enlighten my understanding,
Strengthen my will,
Purify my heart,
and make me holy.

Help me to repent of my past sins
And to resist temptation in the future.
Help me to rise above my human weaknesses
And to grow stronger as a Christian.

Let me love you, my Lord and my God,
And see myself as I really am:
A pilgrim in this world,
A Christian called to respect and love
All whose lives I touch,
Those under my authority,
My friends and my enemies.

Help me to conquer anger with gentleness,
Greed by generosity,
Apathy by fervor.
Help me to forget myself
And reach out toward others.

Make me prudent in planning,
Courageous in taking risks.
Make me patient in suffering,
unassuming in prosperity.

Keep me, Lord, attentive at prayer,
Temperate in food and drink,
Diligent in my work,
Firm in my good intentions.

Let my conscience be clear,
My conduct without fault,
My speech blameless,
My life well-ordered.

Put me on guard against my human weaknesses.
Let me cherish your love for me,
Keep your law,
And come at last to your salvation.

Teach me to realize that this world is passing,
That my true future is the happiness of heaven,
That life on earth is short,
And the life to come eternal.

Help me to prepare for death
With a proper fear of judgment,
But a greater trust in your goodness.
Lead me safely through death
To the endless joy of heaven.

Grant this through Christ our Lord.

Amen.

Pope Clement XI

CHAPTER 7

MICHAL

A woman more concerned with what people might say than with giving God his proper place

It is written: "You shall worship the Lord, your God, and him alone shall you serve."

LUKE 4:8

"Why do you notice the splinter in your brother's eye, but do not perceive the wooden beam in your own?"

LUKE 6:41

"From the fullness of the heart the mouth speaks."

LUKE 6:45

Objective

An excessive concern for "what others will say" is always there in some—if not many—people's lives. This concern rules their lives and decisions and compromises their consciences. In this chapter, we will examine Michal's behavior as a woman who cares more about what others will say—her image—than about giving God his proper place.

Scripture texts: *2 Samuel 6:12–23*
1 Samuel 18:20–29
1 Samuel 19:11–17
1 Samuel 25:44
2 Samuel 3:13–16
1 Chronicles 15:29

Introduction to the character

Who was Michal?

Michal was the daughter of Saul, the first king of Israel, and the wife of David, the second king of Israel. What a privileged place she had in the history of the Hebrew people.

But her actions left much to be desired. Sacred Scripture tells us in the First Book of Samuel how she met David and married him, and in the Second Book of Samuel, we learn about the incident we will study in this chapter: her anger because David praised God by dancing before the Ark of the Lord.

Development of the Bible story

This story begins like many other love stories: "Saul's daughter Michal loved David" (1 Samuel 18:20). What a start: the king's daughter loves the handsome young warrior whom her father despises for having been anointed to succeed him as king of the

Hebrew people. Yet Saul thinks, "I will offer her to him as a trap, so that the hand of the Philistines may strike him" (1 Samuel 18:21). At that time, the Philistines were the staunch enemies of the Hebrew people.

Now it turns out that the father-in-law is giving his daughter, but to set a trap! Sacred Scripture tells us, "Saul feared David all the more and was his enemy ever after. The Philistine chiefs continued to make forays, but each time they took the field, David was more successful against them than any of Saul's other officers, and his name was held in great esteem" (1 Samuel 18:29–30). This is not a very good start, since the father of the bride hates the handsome warrior.

The story continues, telling us that Saul sends some men to David's house to watch him so that he can kill him in the morning. It is then that Michal, his wife, warns him, "Unless you run for your life tonight, tomorrow you will be killed." Then Michal let David down through a window, and he made his escape in safety (1 Samuel 19:11). Michal lays one of the idols she has at home in the bed, putting a tangle of goat's hair at its head and covering it with a blanket. When Saul's men arrive looking for David, she tells them he is sick, and so manages to save her husband's life from her father's hands.

This story is worse than a television program!

The differences continue. David is constantly persecuted by his father-in-law, Saul, who wants to kill him. It then happens that when David has the chance to kill Saul, he stays his hand. Further on, David marries other women while Michal's father gives her to a man named Paltiel.

I know, you are scandalized at all the marriages and are wondering how it is possible that David could have several wives and Michal could have another husband. You will say, "But Jesus said that 'a man shall leave his father and mother [and be joined to his wife] and the two shall become one flesh,' so they are no longer two but one flesh'" (Mark 10:7–8). Let us recall that we are in an era before Jesus and that marriage morality was very different, since people had not yet received the light of revelation that God gave us in Christ.

Continuing, we move on to the Second Book of Samuel, in which we are told in chapter three how David asks Saul's son, Ishbaal, to return his wife Michal to him. Ishbaal "sent for her and took her away from her husband Paltiel" (2 Samuel 3:15).

Finally, we get to the part we will focus on, when David goes out looking for the Ark of the Covenant and, rejoicing, brings it back to Jerusalem, since it represented the presence of God for the Hebrew people.

> As soon as the bearers of the ark of the LORD had advanced six steps, he sacrificed an ox and a fatling. Then David came dancing before the LORD with abandon, girt with a linen ephod. David and all the house of Israel were bringing up the ark of the LORD with shouts of joy and sound of horn.
>
> 2 SAMUEL 6:13–15

It was a great joy for the people and for David: the ark of the Lord had come to their city.

"As the ark of the LORD was entering the City of David, Michal, daughter of Saul, looked down from her window, and when she saw King David jumping and dancing before the LORD, she despised him in her heart" (2 Samuel 6:16). David responds with exultant joy, celebrating the ark's arrival and showing it by dancing, jumping, and leaping. Some Bible translations say he was wearing only a linen ephod, while other translations say he danced naked. It was because of David's expression of joy, which Michal considered exaggerated, that she despised him in her heart.

The feast continues. The ark is brought to the tent that David raised up for it. And it is David himself who offers sacrifices and holocausts and distributes a loaf of bread, a piece of meat, and a raisin cake to all of the people before returning to his home. What a feast!

The time comes for David to return home. Michal is angry and comes out to meet him saying, "How well the king of Israel has honored himself today, exposing himself to the view of the slave girls of his followers, as a commoner might expose himself!" But David replies to Michal: "I was dancing before the LORD. As the LORD lives, who chose me over your father and all his house when he appointed me ruler over the LORD's people, Israel, I will make merry before the LORD" (2 Samuel 6:20–21).

Now David is really in trouble. The lady of the house is angry because she thinks he made a fool of himself in front of the people, dancing, leaping, and doing pirouettes in front of the ark. But David does not see it that way. David thinks he has done the right thing; he has rejoiced in the presence of the Lord and has shown that joy in a patent and visible way. He has praised and worshiped the Lord!

Two people, two ways of seeing things: David sees his actions from the point of view of a believer, while Michal sees them from the human point of view. She is more worried about what people will say than about praising God.

In conclusion, Scripture tells us, "Saul's daughter Michal was childless to the day she died" (2 Samuel 6:23).

What does Michal teach us?

- She teaches us to what extremes a woman can go when she lives constantly concerned about what others will say.
- That her love for David was so deep that she defended him from her own father, helped him escape, and distracted the enemy by putting an idol in the bed. She did everything for him. But she could not stand seeing her husband "making a fool of himself," even for God.
- That self-love can become very strong and can lead us to unthinkable extremes.
- That human respect, the fear of what others will say, dries up, empties, and kills many things.

- That human respect, the fear of what others will say, stops possible initiatives. It paralyzes well-intentioned people.
- That when people are very concerned with what people will say, they are not free. They are slaves of what others may think of them. How many good things are left undone for fear of what people might say?
- That we should give God the first place and let others do likewise.
- That we should respect others.
- To respect others' relationship with God.
- To respect their feelings.
- Not to want to impose our way of thinking on others. Yes, try to lead them to the truth, but respect their freedom along the way.
- That devotion is personal.
- That devotion is translated into action.
- That the purpose of devotion is to honor and revere God.
- That praising God with song, music, and dance is a way of expressing our joy and gratitude to God with all our being.

What does the *Catechism of the Catholic Church* tell us?

§1823: Jesus makes charity the new commandment (see John 13:34). By loving his own "to the end" (John 13:1), he makes manifest the Father's love which he receives. By loving one another, the disciples imitate the love of Jesus which they themselves receive. Whence Jesus says: "As the Father has loved me, so have I loved you; abide in my love" (John 15:9). And again: "This is my commandment, that you love one another as I have loved you" (John 15:12).

§1803: A virtue is a habitual and firm disposition to do the good.

§1804: "Human virtues are firm...attitudes that govern our actions."

§1822: "Charity is the theological virtue by which we love...."

§2097: "To adore God is to acknowledge, in respect and absolute submission, the 'nothingness of the creature' who would not exist but for God. To adore God is to praise and exalt...as Mary did in the Magnificat" in gratitude for all that has been given to each of us and in praise of the holy name of God our Creator.

§2096: To adore God is to acknowledge him as the Creator.

§2135: "Adoring God" is an "act of obedience to the First Commandment."

Questions for personal reflection

- Am I aware that I have countless opportunities in my daily life to do good? Do I use them or let them go by for fear of what people will say?
- Do I understand that I have to make the most of every opportunity to do good?
- Do I strive not to be a victim of the fear of what others will say but instead try to follow the voice of my conscience calling me to do good?
- Is this effort reflected in my resolution to be a better person in all areas of my life, such as in my family, work, and community?
- Have I reflected on how God uses me to reach others' hearts?
- What is my attitude toward people or communities that praise God differently from me? Perhaps they do not sing very well, perhaps they choose to attend Masses that last longer than others or that are in Latin.

- Do I look for the best way to praise God in accordance with my personality, my culture, and my preferences? Or could I not care less whether I praise him or not?
- Have I reflected on how acts of adoration must be an external expression of what I hold inside?
- Do I help out in my parish liturgy?

Group questions and activities

- Reflect on this Gospel passage:

  "Stop judging and you will not be judged. Stop condemning and you will not be condemned. Forgive and you will be forgiven. Give and gifts will be given to you; a good measure, packed together, shaken down, and overflowing, will be poured into your lap. For the measure with which you measure will in return be measured out to you." [...] "Why do you notice the splinter in your brother's eye, but do not perceive the wooden beam in your own? How can you say to your brother, 'Brother, let me remove that splinter in your eye,' when you do not even notice the wooden beam in your own eye? You hypocrite! Remove the wooden beam from your eye first; then you will see clearly to remove the splinter in your brother's eye."

  LUKE 6:37–38, 41–42

- Brainstorm ways we can praise God at church, at home, in private, in the community, etc. How is it possible to praise God in daily life and at all times?
- Make a list of the different cultural and religious traditions we have to praise God. It would be a good idea for someone to note them down, dividing them by countries, and sharing them with more members of the community.
- Think of what could be done to pass on those cultural and religious traditions to the following generations. The ideal would be to make a specific plan.

- Reflect on what the Book of Proverbs tells us: "A good name is more desirable than great riches, and high esteem, than gold and silver" (Proverbs 22:1).

- In Matthew, Jesus says:

  "A wise man built his house on rock. The rain fell, the floods came, and the winds blew and buffeted the house. But it did not collapse; it had been set solidly on rock. And everyone who listens to these words of mine but does not act on them will be like a fool who built his house on sand. The rain fell, the floods came, and the winds blew and buffeted the house. And it collapsed and was completely ruined."

  MATTHEW 7:24–27

  What does the "rock" refer to?

Practical resolutions

- Start the day with a prayer, offering our works to God. May everything we do be for his greater glory and for the good of my brothers and sisters, humankind.
- Be attentive to the material and spiritual needs of those around me, seeking to do good wherever I live.
- Ask the Holy Spirit to help us so we will make the most of our opportunities to do good.
- Read the Gospel every day to know Jesus better and be able to act as he would act.
- Praise God throughout the day in the different circumstances in which we find ourselves.
- Memorize a psalm of praise in order to constantly repeat it.
- Pass on to the following generations our cultural and religious traditions that help us praise God in song, music, and dance.

Prayer

Merciful Father,
You created all humanity
in your image and likeness.
Help us never to judge others.
Remind us that each soul has its motivations
that lead it to act in a specific way,
and that we do not know the reasons for its actions.
If we speak of others, help us to do so
always in a positive way,
and if we have nothing positive to say,
help us to keep quiet.
Take away from our hearts the intention to judge,
from our mouths, the tendency to criticize.
Erase all traces of malice in us, your people,
and by your mercy, create in us, O God,
a pure heart.

You who are infinite love,
fill us with a loving attitude
and never let us separate ourselves from you.
We ask all this in the name of Our Lord Jesus Christ,
who lives and reigns with you for ever and ever.

Amen.

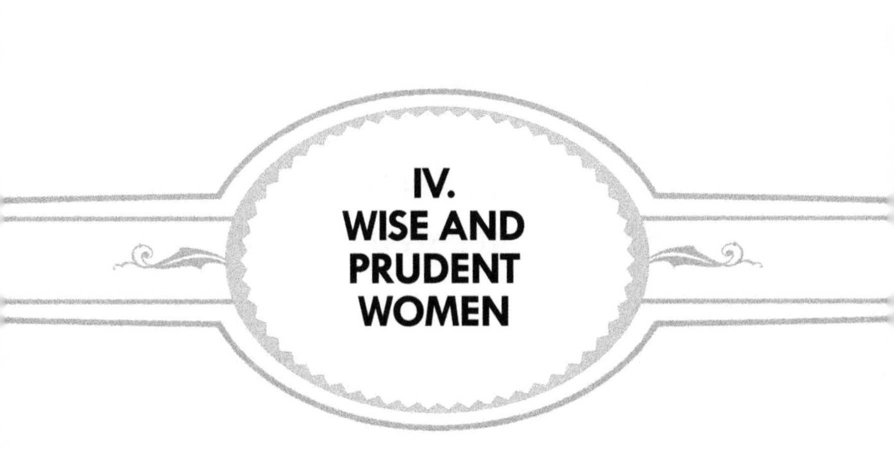

IV. WISE AND PRUDENT WOMEN

CHAPTER 8

HANNAH

A woman of prayer and action

Prayer...is no matter of routine, it is deliberate and earnest. It is not tied down to a fixed timetable; rather it is a state which endures by night and day. Our soul should be directed in God, not merely when we suddenly think of prayer, but even when we are concerned with something else....We should season our actions with the desire and the remembrance of God.

Saint John Chrysostom
Homily 6, on Prayer

Objective

In a society where we dedicate little time to entering into true dialogue with God, Hannah stands out as an example of a woman who puts her trust in God even while going through very difficult circumstances and being misunderstood by those around her.

Scripture text: *1 Samuel 1:1–2, 10; 2:18–21*

Introduction to the character

Who was Hannah?

Hannah's is the story of many women who, through the centuries, have faced the painful reality of wanting to be mothers and not being able to conceive. Hannah was a Hebrew woman, the wife of Elkanah, with whom she traveled up to the sanctuary of Shiloh every year to present her offering and ask the Lord to give her a child.

The beautiful part of this story is that, while she carried a very great sadness, her trust in the Lord was even greater. By the end of the story, we are just as happy as she is. God heard her plea. Months later, Samuel is born, and she consecrates him to the Lord.

Development of the Bible story

The First Book of Samuel begins with the story of Hannah. We see her going up to the sanctuary of Shiloh to worship the Lord and offer sacrifices, just as she does every year. This pilgrimage was a family activity. Scripture tells us that she went with her husband, Elkanah, and his other wife.

Right away, we learn that Hannah had no children because the Lord had made her sterile, while Elkanah's other wife, named Peninnah, did have children. We should bear in mind that our ancestors in the faith saw everything—absolutely everything—as coming from the hand of God, whether it was wealth or poverty, health or sickness, fertility or infertility. Thus, not being able to have children was seen as the will of God.

We also find ourselves with the situation of two women in love with the same man. It is a relationship in which everybody loses, since the human person is made to have one conjugal relationship of total self-giving of the body, mind, will, and feelings. And when this self-giving is not total, everyone suffers. Remember, this story unfolded in the Old Testament during a time when the concept of monogamy was not perceived as clearly as it is today. But we see how, even in that time, where polygamy—usually the marriage of one man with several women—was common and accepted, all of the parties suffered anyway. And here we see that suffering clearly.

In this story, Scripture says Hannah was infertile and that Peninnah humiliated her for it. This only intensified her pain. On the other hand, when it was time to offer sacrifices, Elkanah gave his portions to Peninnah and her children but gave Hannah a double portion because he loved her.

And every year that they made their pilgrimage to the Lord's house, the same thing happened: Peninnah, upon feeling that she was not the favorite, provoked Hannah to irritate her. Hannah wept and stopped eating. Elkanah reacted by saying, "Hannah, why are you weeping? Why are you not eating? Why are you so miserable? Am I not better for you than ten sons?" (1 Samuel 1:8).

On this occasion, Hannah gets up after her meal and goes to the Temple to pray. At that time, the priest Eli sees her and watches her from a distance. "In her bitterness she prayed to the LORD, weeping freely, and made this vow: 'O LORD of hosts, if you look with pity on the hardship of your servant, if you remember me and do not forget me, if you give your handmaid a male child, I will give him to the LORD all the days of his life.

No razor shall ever touch his head'" (1 Samuel 1:10–11).

While she prays before the Lord, Eli sees her lips are moving but that her voice cannot be heard, since Hannah is praying from the depths of her heart. Eli concludes that Hannah is drunk and tells her to leave the Temple.

Poor Hannah, saddened by her infertility, wounded because Elkanah's other wife was mocking her, and now accused of being a drunk! As the saying goes, "When it rains, it pours."

Hannah quickly tells Eli, ""No, my lord! I am an unhappy woman. I have had neither wine nor liquor; I was only pouring out my heart to the LORD. Do not think your servant a worthless woman; my prayer has been prompted by my deep sorrow and misery" (1 Samuel 1:15–16). We can read between the lines that the priest Eli is moved, as he tells her to go in peace with the hope that the God of Israel will grant her request.

Although at first sight, nothing has changed and she continues being sterile, there is a change in Hannah's interior: Now she has hope, and that hope gives her a different attitude. The text tells us she no longer appears downhearted, and that she goes on her way, eats, and the next morning, after worshiping the Lord, her entire family returns home to Ramah, where she has relations with her husband Elkanah. The text tells us that the Lord remembered her.

"When they returned, Elkanah had intercourse with his wife Hannah, and the LORD remembered her. She conceived and, at the end of her pregnancy, bore a son whom she named Samuel. 'Because I asked the LORD for him'" (1 Samuel 1:19–20). Little Samuel is nursed by his mother, and when he is finally weaned, she brings him to the Lord's house and presents him along with a three-year-old bull, an ephah of flour, and a skin of wine. Once the bull is sacrificed, she presents little Samuel to the priest Eli, telling him, "Excuse me, my lord! As you live, my lord, I am the woman who stood here near you, praying to the LORD. I prayed for this child, and the LORD granted my request.

Now I, in turn, give him to the LORD; as long as he lives, he shall be dedicated to the LORD" (1 Samuel 1:26–28).

Hannah concludes her appearance in the Scripture text with a flourish, reciting one of the most beautiful prayers found in the Bible. The prayer is known as Hannah's Canticle:

> My heart exults in the LORD,
> my horn is exalted by my God.
> I have swallowed up my enemies;
> I rejoice in your victory.
>
> There is no Holy One like the LORD;
> there is no Rock like our God.
>
> Speak boastfully no longer,
> Do not let arrogance issue from your mouths.
> For an all-knowing God is the LORD,
> a God who weighs actions.
>
> The bows of the mighty are broken,
> while the tottering gird on strength.
> The well-fed hire themselves out for bread,
> while the hungry no longer have to toil.
> The barren wife bears seven sons,
> while the mother of many languishes.
>
> The LORD puts to death and gives life,
> casts down to Sheol and brings up again.
> The LORD makes poor and makes rich,
> humbles, and also exalts.
>
> He raises the needy from the dust;
> from the ash heap lifts up the poor,
> To seat them with nobles
> and make a glorious throne their heritage.

For the pillars of the earth are the LORD's,
and he has set the world upon them.
He guards the footsteps of his faithful ones,
but the wicked shall perish in the darkness;
for not by strength does one prevail.

The LORD's foes shall be shattered;
the Most High in heaven thunders;
the LORD judges the ends of the earth.
May he give strength to his king,
and exalt the horn of his anointed!

1 SAMUEL 2:1–10

And thus Samuel remained in the service of the Lord.

What does Hannah teach us?

- To be careful with our words, especially when speaking about topics that could hurt others. In Hannah's case, it was infertility. With other people, it could be excess weight, their legal or conjugal situation, perhaps the topic of money, the children, etc.
- Never consciously humiliate another person as Peninnah did. There will be times that we unintentionally hurt someone, but it is one thing to do it without realizing it and another to do it on purpose. That is not right.
- Never fall in love with married men or women. They are already taken and spoken for. Remember that everyone loses with infidelity: the person who falls in love, the spouse, the children, the wife's parents, the husband's parents, the parents of the person who falls in love, and the possible children born of that relationship. Whatever way you look at it, all it brings is suffering.

- Never dismiss the feelings of others. This is what Elkanah did when he told Hannah she had no reason for crying, since he was more than enough for her, better even than ten sons.
- To pray trustingly like Hannah did.
- Never judge without knowing what is really happening, like the priest Eli did. He did not understand that Hannah was praying because she was deeply unhappy, and he even accused her of being drunk!
- To clarify things immediately when there is confusion, as Hannah did with Eli by telling him that she was not a bad woman, but that she was opening her heart to God.
- To live the theological virtue of hope as Hannah did. After presenting her prayer to the Lord, she left at peace, to the point that the text tells us her face changed.
- To be grateful to God.
- To fulfill what we promised to the Lord, as Hannah did. She promised God that if he gave her a son, she would consecrate him to God for the rest of his life. If we promise something to God, we should fulfill it.
- To give God the best we have, as Hannah did. That does not mean that we should go to the parish and hand over our children to the priest. Instead, it means bringing the children to God's house from a young age, teaching them the importance of giving God our best, and of getting them to learn about God from a young age in their religious education classes and at Mass. It means bringing them to the sacrament of reconciliation, to youth activities, etc. It means encouraging them and helping them see the importance and the honor of being able to attend Mass in the house of the Lord.
- To sing the wonders of God.

What does the *Catechism of the Catholic Church* tell us?

The *Catechism of the Catholic Church* dedicates the "fourth part" to Christian prayer. It is recommended we read the section titled "What Is Prayer?" in which it speaks of the universal call to prayer, the prayer of petition, intercession, thanksgiving, praise, and the life of prayer, ending with an extensive explanation of the prayer the Lord taught us: the Our Father.

Below we cite a number from the *Catechism of the Catholic Church* dedicated to the prayer of petition:

§2629: "By prayer of petition we express awareness of our relationship with God. We are creatures who are not our own beginning, not the masters of adversity, not our own last end. We are sinners who as Christians know that we have turned away from our Father. Our petition is already a turning back to him."

Questions for personal reflection

- Do I criticize everything and everyone?
- How much conversation time do I spend talking about others?
- Have I intentionally humiliated anyone? Have I done anything to repair the damage?
- Are there people to whom I owe an apology for having humiliated them? What am I planning to do?
- Do I take others' feelings into account? Always, sometimes, or never?
- Do I put myself in their place? Do I stop to think about what they may be feeling, thinking, where they are coming from, and what they may have suffered beforehand?
- Do I trust in God? Really? Always?

- When something happens in which my attitude or someone else's attitude is misinterpreted, do I clarify it or just let it go? If I let it go, why do I do so? Do I prefer to avoid confrontation?
- Do I live the virtue of hope? Do I really trust in God or do I trust more in my own strengths?
- Have I promised something to God and then not fulfilled it? Why or why not? What am I thinking of doing about it?
- Do I take care of my family's spiritual life? Do I do everything I can so that those closest to me will come to know God? What more can I do?

Group questions and activities

- What have you learned from Hannah, Eli, and Elkanah?
- If you were in the sanctuary of Shiloh when Anna was praying and the priest Eli was speaking to her, what would you give to Anna? How would you console her?
- Compare the Canticle of Hannah (1 Samuel 2:1-10) with the Magnificat (the Canticle of Mary) that the Blessed Virgin recited when she visited her cousin Elizabeth (Luke 1:46–55). How are they similar? How are they different?
- As a group, compose a song of praise to God. You can follow these steps:
  - State the reasons why you want to praise God.
  - One person jots down all the ideas.
  - Together the group composes the canticle.
- Brainstorm ways to help women who are saddened by situations over which they have no control. As in Hannah's case, there was nothing she could do to overcome her infertility.
- Recall and share occasions when you perceived God's answer to your prayers, remembering that God always answers, although not always in the way we want.

- Reflect on what Jesus tells us:

  "Ask and it will be given to you; seek and you will find; knock and the door will be opened to you. For everyone who asks, receives; and the one who seeks, finds; and to the one who knocks, the door will be opened. Which one of you would hand his son a stone when he asks for a loaf of bread, or a snake when he asks for a fish? If you then, who are wicked, know how to give good gifts to your children, how much more will your heavenly Father give good things to those who ask him."

  MATTHEW 7:7–11

Practical resolutions

- Before making a judgment, think about what could have led a person to act as she did. Put yourself in her shoes.
- Always try to speak well of others. If we have nothing good to say, better to say nothing.
- Seek out a person whom you may have humiliated in the past. Talk to her and apologize.
- Strive to take others' feelings into account so that when you speak to them, you do so kindly.
- Make an effort to praise God every day, especially for being your Father and Creator.
- When you have to clarify a situation, do it clearly but charitably.
- Live with hope. Do not let pessimism and despair take over your soul. When you feel despair is getting into your heart, remember that you have the best and most loving of Fathers.
- Read Pope Bendedict XVI's encyclical *Spe Salvi,* on Christian hope.
- Memorize the Magnificat so that you can recite it in moments of difficulty.

Remember,
O most gracious Virgin Mary,
that never was it known
that anyone who fled to thy protection,
implored thy help,
or sought thy intercession
was left unaided.

Inspired with this confidence,
we fly to thee,
O virgin of virgins,
our Mother;
to thee do we come;
before thee we stand,
sinful and sorrowful.

O Mother of the Word Incarnate,
despise not our petitions,
but in thy mercy
hear and answer us.

Amen.

THE MEMORARE

CHAPTER 9

The story of a woman from the Second Book of Maccabees who understood the value of eternal life

"The kingdom of heaven is like a treasure buried in a field, which a person finds and hides again, and out of joy goes and sells all that he has and buys that field. Again, the kingdom of heaven is like a merchant searching for fine pearls. When he finds a pearl of great price, he goes and sells all that he has and buys it. Again, the kingdom of heaven is like a net thrown into the sea, which collects fish of every kind. When it is full they haul it ashore and sit down to put what is good into buckets. What is bad they throw away."

MATTHEW 13:44–48

What eye has not seen, and ear has not heard, and what has not entered the human heart, what God has prepared for those who love him.

1 CORINTHIANS 2:9

Objective

In a world that flees from pain, sadness, and anything uncomfortable and in a world that greatly values gratification in the here and now, this woman is an example of someone who kept her eyes on heaven and her heart set on eternity.

This woman, whose name is not mentioned in sacred Scripture, is presented to us as a model of love for God and of courage. These attitudes originate in the theological virtues of faith, hope, and charity.

Scripture text: *2 Maccabees 7*

Introduction to the character

Who was this mother of seven sons, whose name is not mentioned in sacred Scripture? She appears in the Second Book of Maccabees, chapter seven, in a passage about the martyrdom of seven brothers.

You may be wondering why we are dedicating a chapter of this book to a woman whose name is not even known. The reason is because of her fidelity to God, a fidelity that she was able to inculcate in the hearts of her seven sons. Not only was she faithful, but her sons were as well. This tells us that she was an excellent educator, someone who knew how to teach her sons that obedience to God is the most important thing in life.

Development of the Bible story

The story of this good woman begins in the Second Book of Maccabees with the arrest of the seven brothers, whom the king tried to force to eat pork. The objective was to get them to break the Jewish law, which forbade eating this kind of food. The question arises: Why did the king want this family to break the law? Don't most kings want their citizens to follow the law?

For the answer, we have to go back in time and understand what was happening at that moment in history. The two Books of Maccabees describe a very difficult time period for the Jewish people, since they had been conquered by the biggest and most powerful empire of that time, the Greek Empire.

The Jewish people did not want to be subject to a foreign empire that not only dominated them politically, but also wanted to impose its own way of thinking in religious matters. As a result, the Jews instigated an uprising, which was led by the Maccabees. The Greeks, for their part, persecuted the Jews who insisted on staying faithful to the Jewish law.

In this historical context, the seven brothers are arrested and the king wants them to eat pork so that they will break the Jewish law, the law of Yahweh that forbade them to eat pork.

Upon their arrest, one of the brothers speaks up and tells the king, "What do you expect to learn by questioning us? We are ready to die rather than transgress the laws of our ancestors" (2 Maccabees 7:2). Furious, the king gives orders to have pans and caldrons heated and to cut out the tongue of the one who had spoken for the others, scalp him, cut off his hands and feet, and fry him in the pan. The brothers and their mother encourage one another, saying, "The Lord God is looking on and truly has compassion on us, as Moses declared in his song, when he openly bore witness, saying, 'And God will have compassion on his servants'" (2 Maccabees 7:6).

The second brother is tortured as well, and in his final moments, he tells the king, "You accursed fiend, you are depriving us of this present life, but the King of the universe will raise us up to live again forever, because we are dying for his laws" (2 Maccabees 7:9).

This affirmation of another life is very important. Not everything is in the here and now; there is something more than this life. And the mother understood this very well.

Under torture, the third brother says, "It was from Heaven

that I received these [hands]; for the sake of his laws I disregard them; from him I hope to receive them again" (2 Maccabees 7:11). The king and his court were astonished by the young man's courage.

The torture of the fourth brother follows. Before dying, he says, "It is my choice to die at the hands of mortals with the hope that God will restore me to life; but for you, there will be no resurrection to life" (2 Maccabees 7:14).

We thus see clearly that the mother had sown in her sons' hearts a very deep love for God and his laws, a very great trust in him, and the hope of eternal life, which we normally call heaven. She certainly did a good job. She got her sons to keep their eyes set on heaven. They lived like those who are simply passing through on this earth, knowing that their true homeland is heaven.

Thus we see these brave boys ready to lose their lives in order to save them, as Christ tells us: "If anyone wishes to come after me, he must deny himself and take up his cross daily and follow me. For whoever wishes to save his life will lose it, but whoever loses his life for my sake will save it" (Luke 9:23–24).

Let us continue with the story of this courageous woman and her sons. It is the fifth son's turn to be tortured, but he does not miss the chance to tell the king, "Mortal though you are, you have power over human beings, so you do what you please. But do not think that our nation is forsaken by God. Only wait, and you will see how his great power will torment you and your descendants" (2 Maccabees 7:16–17).

The sixth son's turn comes, and before dying, he tells the king, "Do not think...that you will go unpunished for having dared to fight against God" (2 Maccabees 7:19).

After the death of the sixth son, the author of the Second Book of Maccabees says, "Most admirable and worthy of everlasting remembrance was the mother who, seeing her seven sons perish in a single day, bore it courageously because of her hope in the Lord. Filled with a noble spirit that stirred her womanly reason with manly emotion, she exhorted each of them in the language of their ancestors" (2 Maccabees 7:20–21a). What a woman, truly worthy of admiration! She lost not one, not two or three of her sons, but seven. And of course, in sacred Scripture the number seven signifies plenitude.

The story continues with the mother saying that she does not know how her sons came to be in her womb, that she did not give them breath and life, nor was she the one who arranged the elements of which they were made, but the Creator of the universe himself. Finally, she expresses her confidence in the mercy of God, who will give her sons back both breath and life, "because you now disregard yourselves for the sake of his law" (2 Maccabees 7:23).

But the youngest son is still alive, and the king is quick to get to work so that at least one will renounce his faith. He promises him riches, power, his friendship and happiness, which is something we all want. But the young man pays no heed. Then the king turns to the mother to influence him and convince him to eat the pork and so save his life.

This wise woman accepts the king's invitation to approach her son. Speaking to him in the language of their ancestors, she tells him, "Son, have pity on me, who carried you in my womb for nine months, nursed you for three years, brought you up, educated and supported you to your present age. I beg you, child, to look at the heavens and the earth and see all that is in them; then you will know that God did not make them out of existing things. In the same way humankind came into existence. Do not be afraid of this executioner, but be worthy of your brothers and accept death, so that in the time of mercy I may receive you again with your brothers" (2 Maccabees 7:27–29).

The king thinks that the mother was urging him to renounce his faith so as to save his life, and in reality, she was encouraging him to be faithful to God. The young man declares, "I will not obey the king's command. I obey the command of the law given to our ancestors through Moses. […] Our brothers, after enduring brief pain, have drunk of never-failing life, under God's covenant" (2 Maccabees 7:30, 36). The king is enraged by the boy's words and tortures him even more cruelly than his brothers.

Thus died the young man, in rectitude and total trust in the Lord. Finally, the mother died after her sons (2 Maccabees 7:40–41). With these words, the story and life of the faithful mother come to an end.

What does this woman teach us?

- To love God above all things. This mother fulfilled what Moses asked of the people of God in the Book of Deuteronomy: "This then is the commandment, the statutes and the ordinances, which the LORD, your God, has commanded that you be taught to observe....Hear, O Israel! The LORD is our God, the LORD alone! Therefore, you shall love the LORD, your God, with your whole heart, and with your whole being, and with your whole strength" (Deuteronomy 6:1, 4–5).
- She also teaches us to lead others to love God: "Take to heart these words which I command you today. Keep repeating them to your children. Recite them when you are at home and when you are away, when you lie down and when you get up" (Deuteronomy 6:6–7).
- That there is eternal life and that it is worth making every sacrifice to get there. The Book of Wisdom talks about this: "The souls of the righteous are in the hand of God, and no torment shall touch them" (Wisdom 3:1).
- To have it clear in our mind and heart what it means to go back to God, from whom we came, as the Book of Genesis

tells us: "Then God said: Let us make human beings in our image, after our likeness. Let them have dominion over the fish of the sea, the birds of the air, the tame animals, all the wild animals, and all the creatures that crawl on the earth. God created mankind in his image; in the image of God he created them; male and female he created them" (Genesis 1:26–27).

- That our children are ultimately lent to us. God entrusts them to us so that we can form them and then give them back to him.
- To sow a deep love for God and his commandments in the hearts of our children, our family and friends, and the people who surround us.
- To understand very well that we are not alone on our journey to heaven, and that Jesus is our companion. As he told us before ascending into heaven, "And behold, I am with you always, until the end of the age" (Matthew 28:20).
- Not to get discouraged if we are not quite sure how to get our loved ones to turn their eyes to God, since we have Jesus' promise that if we seek first the kingdom of God and his righteousness, the rest will given to us as well (see Matthew 6:33).
- To imbue our souls and the souls of our children and those around us with the theological virtue of hope. Yes, may all of us learn to hope in God, who is infinite mercy. Let us hope in him, in his help, in his support, in his company alongside us on the journey.
- To understand, as Pope Benedict XVI writes in his encyclical on hope, that God stands in solidarity with us and is especially close to us when sorrow visits us. A God who is close to all humanity: What peace that gives us on our journey!

What does the *Catechism of the Catholic Church* tell us?

§1010: "BecauseofChrist,Christiandeathhasapositivemeaning ....What is essentially new about Christian death is this: through Baptism, the Christian has already 'died with Christ' sacramentally, in order to live a new life."

§992: "God revealed the resurrection of the dead to his people progressively."

§1007: "Death is the end of earthly life."

§1011: At death, the Lord calls all into back to God's own self.

§1013: "There is no 'reincarnation' after death."

§1014: It is important to have a good preparation for the "hour of death."

§1020: Death is an entrance into everlasting life.

§1023: "Those who die in God's grace and friendship and are perfectly purified live forever with Christ."

Questions for personal reflection

- Have I taken seriously the commandment to "love God above all things?" Really?
- What comes first: my likes and whims, my comfort, or God?
- Do I think it is important to reach heaven at the end of my life? Why?
- Do I act like someone who wants to get to heaven? Or like someone who wants to get to heaven "only sometimes?"
- Have I taught others to love God above all things? Have I done so with my words, example, or both?
- Have I taken seriously my role as an educator of my children, nieces, and nephews, etc.?
- Am I aware that Jesus is my companion on the journey? That I am truly not alone on my journey to heaven?
- What can I do to value the greatness of eternal life with God more deeply? What do I need to understand that it is something wonderful, since I was created for it?
- What can I do to help others value the greatness of eternal life with God more deeply?

Group questions and activities

- Analyze why there are people today who live as if eternal life did not exist and why the "here and now" attracts them more.
- Brainstorm what you can do to reach eternal life. In a brain-storm-ing session, all participants give their ideas and some-one writes them down; all ideas are welcome, and no one is criticized or belittled. At the end, the list is read, letting the Holy Spirit act in each soul. He knows which of the ideas apply to each person's life.
- Do another brainstorming session on the topic: What can I do to get my loved ones to reach eternal life? Follow the in-structions given in the previous point.
- Look for passages in sacred Scripture about eternal life or the kingdom of heaven.
- Reflect on the following passage from the Book of Wisdom 3:1–10:

  The souls of the righteous are in the hand of God, and no torment shall touch them. They seemed, in the view of the foolish, to be dead; and their passing away was thought an affliction and their going forth from us, utter destruction. But they are in peace. For if to others, indeed, they seem punished, yet is their hope full of immortality. Chastised a little, they shall be greatly blessed, because God tried them and found them worthy of himself. As gold in the furnace, he proved them, and as sacrificial offerings he took them to himself. In the time of their judgment they shall shine and dart about as sparks through stubble. They shall judge nations and rule over peoples, and the LORD shall be their King forever. Those who trust in him shall understand truth, and the faithful shall abide with him in love: Because grace and mercy are with his holy ones, and his care is with the elect. But the wicked shall receive a punishment to match their thoughts, since they neglected righteousness and forsook the LORD.

- The most valuable possession of a follower of Christ is friendship with him, but there are some attitudes that endanger that friendship. Make a list of the attitudes that can endanger our life of grace, that is, our friendship with God. Some examples: bad friendships, readings, television programs, Web pages, etc. Afterward, write down some concrete ways to take care of the life of grace or friendship with God in the face of these situations.

Practical resolutions

- During your prayer times, thank God for those times when you believed in him, obeyed his teachings and lived with the hope that he is your Father and you are in his hands.
- Ask God forgiveness for those times when you have behaved as if you did not believe in him or as if he did not matter to you.
- They say the best way to learn to swim is by swimming. The same holds true for the faith: The best way to believe in God and believe God is by living as if you believed in him, totally abandoned into his hands.
- Always seek out means like prayer and the sacraments to help you be a better friend of God.
- Be aware of how important it is to live in the state of grace, in friendship with God. And if for some reason you lose it, resolve to go to the sacrament of reconciliation.
- Ask the Holy Spirit to help you keep your friendship with God.
- Live every day as if it were the last day of your life.
- Do everything you can to share what you learned in this chapter with those around you.

Prayer for the children

Father of goodness,
We come before you praying with our whole hearts
for you to protect the children that you,
in your infinite goodness, have given to us.
We know that they came from you,
and that we must help them come back to you.
Do not let them offend you
with their thoughts, actions, or words.
Take care of them in this life;
keep them close to your heart,
and at the end of their days,
lead them to rejoice in your presence.
We pray for our smallest children, your little ones:
protect their innocence.
For our teenage children:
be their companion during this stage of their lives.
For our adult children: may they come to you
before making the big decisions of this stage in life.
Help us, Lord, to know how to bring them to you,
and may they find guidance and strength,
affection and shelter in us.
Forgive our weaknesses, make up for what we lack.
And call us to come to you, so that with your angels and saints, we may praise you eternally.
We ask all this in the name of our Lord, Jesus Christ.

Amen.

CHAPTER 10

THE WOMAN OF PROVERBS 31

Who can find a woman of worth?
Far beyond jewels is her value.
Her husband trusts her judgment;
he does not lack income.
She brings him profit, not loss,
all the days of her life.
She reaches out her hands to the poor,
and extends her arms to the needy.
She is clothed with strength and dignity,
and laughs at the days to come.
She opens her mouth in wisdom;
kindly instruction is on her tongue.
She watches over the affairs of her household,
and does not eat the bread of idleness.
Her children rise up and call her blessed;
her husband, too, praises her:
"Many are the women of proven worth,
but you have excelled them all."
Charm is deceptive and beauty fleeting;
the woman who fears the LORD is to be praised.

PROVERBS 31:10–12, 20, 25–30

Objective

We live in a society where many people are valued not for who they are, but for what they have: beauty, grace, fame, power, success, money, material possessions, etc.

This chapter's goal is to teach us to see people, both men and women, as God sees them. It is about understanding that their value comes from being a creature of God and that the knowledge, material possessions, and other things we acquire in this world are just means to become what we are called to be.

Scripture text: *Proverbs 31:10–31*

Introduction to the character

Who was the woman of Proverbs 31?

The woman of Proverbs 31 is not a biblical character as such. Proverbs 31 speaks to us of a woman who uses the qualities God gave her for good.

This chapter will be different from the others: Instead of talking about this woman, we will study what sacred Scripture says about how the human person should behave, so that we can learn and then apply it to our own lives.

We can ask ourselves: What did God give me? Perhaps a joyful or energetic personality, perhaps a good sense of humor, or the capacity to be strong in the face of adversity; or perhaps leadership skills or a good work ethic. And then we can ask ourselves: What am I doing with the gifts God gave me? How am I putting them at the service of God and the community so that at the end of my life I will hear, "Well done, my good and faithful servant. Since you were faithful in small matters, I will give you great responsibilities. Come, share your master's joy." (Matthew 25:23)?

In short, this chapter will be highly practical, and it is put at the end of the book on purpose so that, after reading about and studying the women of the Old Testament, we will go out into the world and fulfill Christ's missionary mandate: "Go, therefore, and make disciples of all nations, baptizing them in the name of the Father, and of the Son, and of the Holy Spirit, teaching them to observe all that I have commanded you. And behold, I am with you always, until the end of the age" (Matthew 28:19–20). We will do this by using the gifts God gave us.

Development of the Bible story

In this case, there is not a story *per se*, but a description of how a woman—or any human being, for that matter—should be.

With this section of chapter thirty-one, the Book of Proverbs comes to a conclusion. It has been described in various ways: "poem in honor of the perfect woman," "eulogy to the industrious woman," "a good housewife," "a woman of noble character," "the ideal wife," "acrostic to an exemplary woman," etc. The common denominator to all of these names is the appreciation for a woman's ideal behavior.

Proverbs contains an enormous treasury of teachings to help people behave appropriately in different situations. It belongs to the literary genre of the Wisdom Books, whose purpose is to offer teachings or instructions on living wisely. It aims to instruct and make us reflect on the right way of acting in life so that we become what God wants us to be.

Thus, in this chapter, we will try to describe what God wants of each one of us in the state and condition of life to which we have been called.

What does the woman of Proverbs 31 teach us?

We can glean great teachings from this Scripture passage. But first we need to reflect on how we see ourselves, recognizing our qualities and accepting our limitations. Then we must try to understand how God sees us so we can discover the loving hands of God in our lives. Lastly, we must ask him to help us be the type of person he wants us to be.

How do I see myself?

- As a child of God?
- As a member of the big family of the Church?
- Sad, blessed, taken care of, applauded, celebrated, accompanied through life, alone, embittered, hopeful, drifting, living by whatever comes my way, committed to my responsibilities, respected, helpless, confrontational, patient, peaceful, loving, feeling exposed, secure, insecure, wounded, yearning, optimistic, tired, trusting, enthusiastic, ugly, attractive, very fat, very short, very tall, very happy...?
- How do I live my life?
- Do I live it as if it were wasted, pointless time?
- Am I aware that I have only one life and that time is passing by?
- Am I aware that with every day that passes by, I am a day closer to eternal life?
- How do I react to difficulties?

How does God see me?

- As his child?
- As a product of his creation?
- As a work of art come forth from his loving hands?
- As a beautiful masterpiece?
- As an expression of his infinite wisdom?
- As a unique and unrepeatable being for whom he created the world and everything in it?

Yes, I must see myself for what I am: a creature of God, come forth from his loving hands. A human life that, no matter the ups and downs, was created by a God who does not make mistakes. A life that perhaps needs to be put in line with what the Lord asks of us, but that is what the sacraments are for. Let us go to the sacrament of reconciliation, let us make an examination of conscience, let us be sorry for having offended God. Let us tell the priest our sins and after making a firm resolution not to offend God anymore, let us do our penance. And let us receive Christ in the sacrament of the Eucharist.

- After reflecting on the points above, we can move on to the next steps:
  - Find the loving hand of God in every circumstance of my life.
  - In my first years of life.
  - In my current circumstances.
  - In my relationships with others.
  - Even in my sorrows, problems, sufferings, and illnesses. God is also there.

And finally:
Ask God to make us the people he wants us to be.

Ask him to make us, his children, capable of putting at his service and at the service of my fellow brothers and sisters in all my capacities to be that "worthy," "ideal," "industrious," "noble," "exemplary" person, as described in Proverbs 31.

What does the *Catechism of the Catholic Church* tell us?

§27: "The desire for God is written in the human heart, because" we are "created by God and for God."

§30: God continues calling humanity.

§33: Concerning the human person and the existence of God

§68: "By love, God" reveals to humanity the personhood of God's own self: namely the Blessed Trinity.

§142: Revelation unveils the invisible God, inviting humanity into the fullness of divine life.

§143: Men and women are called to entrust their wills to that of their Creator in faith.

§229: Faith leads us to God.

§231: God is "abounding in steadfast love and faithfulness" (Exodus 34:6).

§268: God is omnipotent.

§271: "God's almighty power is in no way arbitrary."

§274: "Nothing is impossible for God."

§278: We should have faith in the love of God.

§295: "God created the world" in infinite and divine "wisdom."

Questions for personal reflection

- Am I capable of loving, sacrificing myself, being joyful, laughing, making others happy, giving generously, working joyfully, working even when it's hard for me, serving, healing others' bodies and souls, helping those in need, encouraging, teaching, guiding, giving hope, praying, consoling, smiling, showing by my example that life is worth living, living with gusto, singing, whistling, working for something worthwhile?
- Make a list of my qualities. I most definitely have something good to share with others.
- A list of qualities is presented below as a guide, although it is necessarily incomplete.
  - Adaptable
  - Affectionate
  - Analytical
  - Balanced
  - Compassionate
  - Conciliatory
  - Creative
  - Determined
  - Disciplined
  - Energetic
  - Enthusiastic
  - Even-tempered
  - Faithful
  - Farsighted
  - Fighter
  - Flexible
  - Frank
  - Friendly
  - Good listener
  - Happy
  - Hard-working
  - Helpful
  - Honest
  - Ingenious
  - Intellectual
  - Intelligent
  - Joyful
  - Kind
  - Knowledgeable
  - Leader
  - Logical
  - Loving
  - Loyal
  - Mature

- Merciful
- Optimistic
- Organized
- Persevering
- Pious
- Practical
- Prudent
- Punctual
- Responsible
- Secure
- Spirited
- Spiritual
- Stable
- Studious
- Team player
- Tenacious
- Trustworthy
- Understanding
- Upright

Group questions and activities

- Brainstorm about "true happiness." What gives true happiness? Remember that all ideas are valid and none should be rejected. A member of the group takes notes and reads the list at the end.
- Feelings are good and they allow us to relate to others, but when they control us instead of us controlling them, they become a problem, since we become their slaves. How can you avoid letting yourself be carried away by feelings?
- What can we do to put all of our capacities to be a "worthy," "ideal," "industrious," "noble," or "exemplary" man or woman, as described in Proverbs 31, at the service of God and our fellow man?
- Reflect on the following statement: "A 'good' life does not mean feeling happy all the time. A good life comes from living before God."

Practical resolutions

This book has come to its end. In order to help you apply the lessons you may have learned, I would like to make some simple suggestions:

1. Keep a journal. A journal will help you understand:
   - What you have gone through.
   - Your sufferings.
   - What gives you joy.
   - When you are most vulnerable.
   - What makes you uncomfortable.

   It will help you to see:
   - How far you have come.
   - Your progress as a person.
   - Your spiritual progress.
   - The good experiences you have had.
   - That in spite of many obstacles, you are here...alive, ready to carry on.

   It will give you a historical perspective on what you have experienced, felt, appreciated, confronted, and endured.
   - To celebrate the good.
   - To admit, repair, and change the bad.

2. Look for a model to follow. Find someone worth imitating, a person who leaves the good "aroma of Christ" in his or her wake, as Saint Paul says in the Second Letter to the Corinthians.

3. Choose the environment where you will live and move.
    - Pay more attention to the people around you.
    - Invest your time in cultivating good friendships and frequenting the people or groups who bring out the best in you.
4. Choose to be a good person.
    - Make a conscious choice: "I want to be a good person," and I am going to apply the means to achieve it.
    - I will be a good person always, at every moment.
    - I will be aware that my face belongs to others.
    - I will give others the benefit of the doubt.
    - I will always think well of others.
    - I will never speak badly of them.
5. Take charge of your life. Your life is up to you.
    - There are sufferings from the past that can inhibit or paralyze you. Don't let them in. They belong to the past.
    - Get out of that circle of pain, misunderstanding, and nightmare.
    - Understand that the more you go back into the same furrow, the deeper the wound will get.
6. Live charity
    - Live moral, ethical, and religious values.
    - You wonder: How do I do that?
    - See how other people you respect behave.
    - Read positive things. Saint Ignatius of Loyola's conversion began when he read the lives of the saints.
    - Attend faith formation classes and Bible studies where you can learn more about God, his love, his grace, and your fellow man.

- Go to groups at church. There you will find people who want to follow the Lord more closely.

7. Change your attitude.
    - Of course it is hard. If things were easy, anyone would do them.
    - No matter what it costs...change.
    - You have to endure the pain that comes with change; any change will be tough.
8. Live by and for God and others.
    - Live for something and someone other than yourself.
    - Stop wanting to be the center of attention all the time.
    - Enough of always being the victim.
    - It will not be easy. They will unintentionally hurt you, you will suffer, and you will have a hard time.
    - Start giving to others, especially your husband, children, neighbors, strangers, the community, city, and country.

Prayer

Lord, make me an instrument of your peace.
Where there is hatred, let me sow love;
where there is injury, pardon;
where there is doubt, faith;
where there is despair, hope;
where there is darkness, light;
and where there is sadness, joy.

O Divine Master, grant that I may not so much seek
to be consoled as to console;
to be understood as to understand;
to be loved as to love.
For it is in giving that we receive;
it is in pardoning that we are pardoned;
and it is in dying that we are born to eternal life. Amen.

Saint Francis of Assisi

CPSIA information can be obtained
at www.ICGtesting.com
Printed in the USA
LVHW01s2304291217
561286LV00009B/141/P